Hypnosis & Hypnotherapy

what you need to know

GARY ELKINS, PHD

CAMERON ALLDREDGE, PHD

Published by:
Mountain Pine Publishing
Waco, Texas

Hypnosis and Hypnotherapy: What You Need to Know
Copyright 2024 by Gary Elkins, PhD and Cameron Alldredge, PhD
and individual contributors

ISBN: 979-8-218-58105-3

All rights reserved. Without limiting the rights under copyright reserved above, no part of this publication may be reproduced, stored in or introduced into a retrieval system, or transmitted, in any form, or by any means (electronic, mechanical, photocopying, recording, or otherwise) without the prior written permission of both the copyright owner and the above publisher of this book.

Contents

Acknowledgments i
Contributors iii
Try It Yourself: Online Access to Free Self-Hypnosis Resources v
Introduction 1
Chapter 1:   What Is Hypnosis and Hypnotherapy? 3
Chapter 2:   How Does Hypnotherapy Work? 13
Chapter 3:   What Happens During a Hypnotherapy Session? 21
Chapter 4:   Is Hypnosis Safe? 27
Chapter 5:   How Popular Is Hypnotherapy? 33
Chapter 6:   Hypnotherapy: What the Science Says 41
Chapter 7:   How Do I Know if I Can Be Hypnotized? 49
Chapter 8:   Smoking Cessation 57
Chapter 9:   Menopause and Women's Health:
             Hot Flashes and Sleep 67
Chapter 10: Sleep and Insomnias 79
Chapter 11: Trauma and PTSD 91
Chapter 12: Irritable Bowel Syndrome 97
Chapter 13: Stress Management 107
Chapter 14: Fears and Phobias 113
Chapter 15: Anxiety and Depression 123
Chapter 16: Chronic Pain 133
Chapter 17: Mindfulness and Hypnosis 141
Chapter 18: Weight Management 149
Chapter 19: Coping with Cancer 157
Chapter 20: Coping with Medical Procedures 167
Chapter 21: Sports and Performance 173

Chapter 22: Flow State and Hypnosis ... 181
Chapter 23: What Is Stage Hypnosis And How Does It Work? ... 187
Chapter 24: Beginning Hypnotherapy and Additional Resources ... 191
Concluding Remarks ... 197
About the Authors ... 201

Acknowledgments

I wish to acknowledge the individuals who contributed to the chapters in this book for their dedication and expertise. Also, Meredith Vagner for her reading, review, and formatting of chapters, Michael Vinson for his review, and Elizabeth Beeton for her assistance and manuscript preparation. A book of this nature takes many hours of time and effort. I am eternally grateful to my lovely wife, Guillerma Elkins, for her guidance and amazing support.

Gary Elkins, PhD

•••

I wish to acknowledge the excellent mentorship I've received from Dr. Elkins in the years leading up to the production of this book. His guidance and direction during these formative years of my career have been indispensable. I deeply appreciate my friends and co-authors with whom I work alongside every day. Finally, I wish to express love and gratitude to my wife, Megan, and our three children Lili, Violet, and Cooper for their unwavering love and support.

Cameron Alldredge, PhD

Contributors

The Mind-Body Medicine Research Laboratory at Baylor University stands as one of the world-leading research labs for clinical hypnosis. We (Drs. Elkins and Alldredge) lead the lab which conducts hypnosis research and publishes many scientific articles each year across a wide variety of hypnosis-related topics. Within the lab, we mentor 10 doctoral students (of both clinical and experimental psychology) and about a dozen undergraduate research assistants. The co-authors on many of the chapters are current students in the lab and assisted in the writing of this book in many important ways. Their authorship is indicated for each chapter, and they are acknowledged here.

Chris Corlett, MA
PhD Student

Vindhya Ekanayake, MS, MSCP
PsyD Student

Alex Hood, BA
PsyD Student

Aaron Finley, MSCP
PsyD Student

Vanessa Muñiz, MA
PhD Student

Victor Julian Padilla, ScM
PhD Student

Skyla Renner-Wilms, MS, MSCP
PsyD Student

Katherine Scheffrahn, BS
PhD Student

Katie Seidenberg, BS
PsyD Student

Meredith Vagner
Undergraduate Research Assistant

Michael Vinson, MSCP
PsyD Student

TRY IT YOURSELF

The best way to learn about hypnosis is to experience it for yourself.

To get the most out of this self-hypnosis experience, you should:
1. Find a place where you feel safe and will not be disturbed.
2. Sit or lie down with good support for your head, neck, and shoulders.
3. Have an open and non-judgmental attitude of acceptance.

**FREE SELF-HYPNOSIS
SESSIONS AVAILABLE AT:**

www.mindsethealth.com/hypnosisbonus

Introduction

Despite a wealth of scientific study spanning decades, hypnosis remains mysterious to much of the general population. Its portrayal (or misrepresentation) through media and live entertainment has led many to wonder whether hypnosis is a real thing. We don't blame anyone for being skeptical of hypnosis. Instead, we simply view unbelief in hypnosis as an indication that someone doesn't know what it is or how it works.

We wrote this book to fill a gap we noticed in books about hypnosis. We are familiar with many of the wonderful books written by well-educated psychologists and experts on the clinical use of hypnosis. These books are great for professionals who want to integrate hypnosis into their practice. We are also aware that many of the books written for the general public are not grounded in the scientific literature of hypnosis, and their content can be misleading. Thus, our goal for this book was to create a resource that is 1) rooted in the science, but 2) intended to be read by everyday people and healthcare providers unfamiliar with clinical hypnosis.

In this book, we present scientific findings on hypnosis and hypnotherapy as they have emerged from empirical research (such as randomized clinical trials and neuroimaging studies) conducted at major universities. We explain how hypnotherapy can be a powerful source of help, is easy to practice, and has many applications. We separate the reality from the "hype" and cover *what the science says* about hypnosis. As licensed psychologists who regularly use hypnotherapy in our private practice, we also outline how hypnotherapy works, what to expect from a hypnosis session, its safety, hypnotizability, and practical tips for trying self-hypnosis.

We have personally seen many amazing things accomplished with the use of clinical hypnosis. However, we recognize that hypnotherapy is not a magical cure for all problems. While hypnotherapy can help with many things, it does take effort and motivation. In essence, hypnosis can help you learn to experience a special state of consciousness, gain greater access to your unconscious mind, and become open and able to respond to positive therapeutic suggestions. Further, the practice of self-hypnosis can be integrated into daily life to accomplish personal goals.

Hypnotherapy can help to increase your confidence, build stronger self-esteem, and create a sense of empowerment in dealing with life's challenges. It can be used by itself or in combination with medical treatments and psychotherapy. Interestingly, many studies have shown that hypnotherapy boosts the effectiveness of other treatments when they are combined. Hypnotherapy will deepen your understanding of the mind-body connection and how it can be used for health and well-being.

This book is organized along several themes. The first few chapters cover the definitions of hypnosis and hypnotherapy, how hypnotherapy works, and a broad overview of scientific evidence. This is followed by chapters on hypnotherapy for specific issues which will summarize the science and provide an idea about how hypnotherapy can help. The final chapters address stage hypnosis, finding a hypnotherapist, digital health apps, and resources for more information.

If we are successful in our goal for this book, readers will walk away with a clear and scientific understanding of what hypnosis is, how hypnotherapy can help, and what to do next in trying it for themselves. At the end of each chapter, we include a list of references and sources which can provide even more information. With that, let's begin with Chapter 1 and answer the question, *what is hypnosis and hypnotherapy*?

Chapter 1
What Is Hypnosis and Hypnotherapy?

GARY ELKINS

CAMERON ALLDREDGE

Hypnosis and hypnotherapy have a lot in common with other mind-body practices such as guided meditation, mindfulness, and relaxation response training. Each of these methods can lead to certain states of consciousness that involve focus, visualization, and acceptance of positive suggestions for specific goals. Psychologists and medical researchers have shown that these special states of consciousness, combined with therapeutic suggestions and guided imagery, can reduce stress, improve well-being, and help with making positive changes in many areas (such as smoking cessation, sleep, anxiety, depression, irritable bowel syndrome, menopausal symptoms, emotional regulation, and pain management). In this chapter, you will discover exactly what hypnosis is and the 10 key principles of hypnotherapy.

Where Does the Word "Hypnosis" Come From?

The word *hypnosis* was first used around the year 1850 by a Scottish physician named James Braid. During his treatment with some patients, Dr. Braid had them focus on an object and gave them instructions for relaxation and "sleep." In the early years of his practice, Dr. Braid mistakenly thought his patients were asleep during the treatment. Because of this, he used the Greek word *hypnos* (meaning "sleep") to invent the term "hypnotism" which evolved into the word "hypnosis." However, he later realized that sleep and the hypnotic state are different. He even tried to rename hypnosis as "monoideism" (focusing on a single thought) which clearly wasn't as catchy. Even though the field of modern hypnosis also recognizes that it is not the same as sleep, the term *hypnosis* has persisted through the centuries and remains the word we use today.

What is the Definition of Hypnosis?

Since the time of James Braid, there have been various perspectives and misperceptions about hypnosis. For this reason, the American Psychological Association's Division of Psychological Hypnosis came out with this definition in 2015:

> ***"Hypnosis is a state of consciousness involving focused attention and reduced peripheral awareness, characterized by an enhanced capacity for response to suggestion."***

If we break that definition down, there are three main parts:

1. *Focused attention* simply means that a person's thoughts are intently on one thing.
2. *Reduced peripheral awareness* refers to the idea that a person isn't as concerned about other things that may be going on around them.
3. *Enhanced capacity for response to suggestion* means that suggestions are accepted much easier than usual. Suggestions may refer to something you think, feel, or do.

This is something you have probably experienced many times before. For example, a lot of people can become completely absorbed in a good movie or novel. It's almost as if they enter the reality of the story being told and start to feel what the characters might be feeling. This is the very reason why books and movies are so popular—they can lead people to feel and experience things like romance, suspense, joy, connection, or horror. Just like our definition of hypnosis, people absorbed in a novel or movie are 1) completely focused on the story, 2) not aware of or concerned with other things going on around them, and 3) can feel and experience the story as if it were 100% real and happening to them. Similar to what happens in hypnosis, an important part of experiencing a book or movie is that *critical judgment* is suspended. This refers to the fact that you are likely not enjoying a great action film while simultaneously thinking "this is just a highly paid actor wearing makeup running around in front of a green screen with a film crew." Like in hypnosis, the experience being suggested is openly accepted without critical judgment.

We would like to emphasize here that hypnosis is not something that is *done to you*, but rather something that you *learn to experience*. Hypnosis is a natural and normal state of consciousness that we all have the capacity to experience and use. Everyone has experienced hypnosis to some degree (even if you didn't call it that!) and anyone can benefit from hypnotherapy.

What is the Definition of Hypnotherapy?

At the same time the Division of Psychological Hypnosis came out with their definition of hypnosis, they also provided a definition for *hypnotherapy* which is **"the use of hypnosis in the treatment of a medical or psychological disorder or concern."** Hypnotherapy simply refers to the use of hypnosis to achieve a particular goal or purpose. Hypnosis + therapy = hypnotherapy. Sometimes hypnotherapy is delivered by an individual provider, but it can also be delivered using *self-*

hypnosis (discussed more later) which may involve audio recordings or a hypnosis app.

The 10 Key Principles of Hypnotherapy

Hypnotherapy has several foundational principles. You can think of these as a kind of theory or as basic beliefs that guide our understanding of hypnosis and hypnotherapy.

1. **Hypnosis is a natural state of consciousness.**
   Thanks to our human brain, we all have the ability to focus our attention, become absorbed in an activity, experience mental imagery, and be open to positive suggestions. This is a natural ability. Most people discover on their own that they can create a deeply relaxed state of consciousness and have vivid mental experiences. This can be useful in dealing with stress or pain (such as going to the dentist) or reinforcing positive "self-talk."

2. **Hypnotherapy is most effective when a person is motivated and has positive expectancies.**
   In a sense, *all hypnosis is self-hypnosis,* which means that no one can be "hypnotized against their will." We respond best to hypnotherapy when it is for something that we are motivated to change or achieve. Having a positive expectancy means being open to the experience and anticipating that good things can occur from the hypnotherapy and practice of self-hypnosis.

3. **Hypnotherapy is directed toward empowering a person.**
   When clinicians use hypnosis, the goal is to help the client achieve what the client wants to achieve. The goal is empowerment. For instance, if you want to learn how to

use hypnosis to stop smoking or reduce stress, you will be empowered as you achieve your goals. This is why most hypnotherapy involves teaching the client how to do self-hypnosis; by learning self-hypnosis, a person is empowered to become their own hypnotherapist which can be used in many ways (e.g., reducing stress, sleeping better, managing pain, visualizing goals).

4. **Hypnotherapists recognize there are individual differences in hypnotizability.**
   Everyone has the capability of experiencing hypnosis. However, it has long been recognized that people vary in how well they can experience hypnosis and respond to suggestions. These individual differences are referred to as differences in *hypnotizability*. Hypnotizability can be thought of as a trait or talent that we all possess to varying degrees. The trait of hypnotizability is like intellectual ability in that both are stable traits (they do not change much over time) and those that have a high intellectual ability can usually learn to do things more quickly than others. Likewise, the person who is high in hypnotizability possesses an ability to experience and use hypnosis quickly to mobilize the mind-body connection. People who are lower in hypnotizability have the same abilities but may need more sessions or to practice self-hypnosis more often to achieve the same results.

5. **All communication is processed within both the conscious and unconscious mind.**
   Many psychologists believe that there are two systems in the brain that work to process information. The first is often referred to as the *conscious mind*. This is the system that processes information logically and analytically, and it doesn't deal much with emotions. The second system is the

unconscious mind which processes information through imagery, feelings, and intuition. It processes through the lens of personal experience and is more emotionally driven. Many psychologists believe that a lot of what influences our feelings and behavior is unconscious—that is, we don't have to consciously think about them. Hypnotic suggestions are generally directed toward the unconscious mind which can be very powerful in changing thoughts, feelings, and actions.

6. **A state of hypnosis can make it easier to experience positive suggestions.**
Hypnotherapy relies on the use of *hypnotic suggestions*. Suggestions are not instructions, but rather invitations for changes in thoughts, feelings, physiology, and behaviors. Of course, we can respond to suggestions without hypnosis—that happens all the time. Suggestions, however, are foundational to hypnotherapy because a person can easily experience suggested effects after a hypnotic induction intended to bring about the state of consciousness we call *hypnosis.*

7. **Hypnotherapy sessions are goal-directed.**
The content of specific hypnotic suggestions depends entirely upon the goal of the session. For example, hypnotherapy for improvement in sport performance typically involves mental imagery for focus, success, determination, endurance, and relaxation, whereas hypnotherapy for pain management usually involves hypnotic suggestions for analgesia, numbness in an area of the body, or non-judgmental acceptance of physical discomforts. Whatever the intended goal happens to be, the suggestions are designed and crafted around that.

8. **Hypnotherapy sessions may be both structured and individualized.**
    Built upon decades of research, hypnotherapy has increasingly become an *evidenced-based treatment*. Much of the structure and content of hypnotherapy sessions may be based upon clinical research and established protocols. At the same time, it is recognized that everyone is unique—what works for one person may not work the same way for another. Therefore, hypnotherapy usually involves sessions that consider the individual's past experiences and integrates their preferences for mental imagery and wording of suggestions.

9. **Hypnotherapy is integrative.**
    It is important to know that hypnotherapy usually involves multiple components such as education, homework assignments for personal practice, interpersonal support, and behavioral modifications. Hypnotherapy may be a "stand-alone" therapy, or it may be used in combination with medications or another type of psychotherapy such as cognitive-behavioral therapy (CBT). Research has shown that combining hypnotherapy with CBT generally achieves greater benefits than CBT by itself.

10. **Hypnotherapy may be directed toward developing coping skills, relieving symptoms, facilitating insight, or preventing relapse.**
    Hypnotherapy has many uses. Like CBT or mindfulness training, it can be used to develop coping skills. This can include learning how to relax and cope with pain or stressful situations. In other cases, hypnotherapy intends to relieve specific symptoms. An example is using hypnotherapy to treat hot flashes in menopause. Extensive research supports the fact that hypnotherapy can be used to achieve a

significant reduction in the intensity and number of hot flashes experienced—not just better coping with them (as is the case with mindfulness and CBT). Hypnotherapy can also be used to uncover unconscious feelings or perceptions. This is especially important in facilitating insight as it may relate to depression, anxiety, fear, or even smoking cessation. Finally, once goals are achieved, it is important to maintain the improvements. Hypnotherapy is often used to prevent returning to old habits and past lifestyles. For example, hypnotherapy can help to prevent regaining lost weight or having future panic attacks.

Equipped with this foundational knowledge of hypnosis and hypnotherapy, we hope that both patients and clinicians can make a more informed decision about using hypnotherapy and referring it to others.

Hypnotherapy Isn't a Magic Cure

As we mentioned previously, hypnotherapy is not so much something that is done to you, as it is something that you learn to experience. People who expect to sit in a hypnotherapist's office and have a problem "hypnotized away" without any additional practice or action on their part will probably be disappointed. Mobilizing the power of hypnotherapy and your hypnotic abilities takes persistence, confidence, and daily practice. Hypnotherapy is a unique and empowering experience. The response to hypnotic suggestions for relaxation and the acceptance of positive ideas can *feel* effortless, but it is not a magic cure. Making changes takes effort, practice, and determination.

Summary

Hypnosis is a state of consciousness involving focused attention and reduced peripheral awareness, characterized by an enhanced capacity for response to suggestion. It is a natural state of consciousness that, when used for a therapeutic purpose, is called hypnotherapy. Everyone is hypnotizable to some degree, and anyone can benefit from hypnotherapy. However, it is not a magic cure. Hypnotherapy follows 10 key principles that inform our understanding of using hypnosis therapeutically. When hypnotherapy is combined with high motivation and personal practice, it can help mobilize the *mind-body connection* to help someone stop smoking, manage menopause symptoms, lose weight, treat trauma, minimize fears, improve IBS, reduce stress and anxiety, and manage pain (as well as many other uses that we will cover throughout the book).

REFERENCES

Elkins, G. (2017). *Handbook of medical and psychological hypnosis: Foundations, applications, and professional issues.* Springer Publishing Co.

Elkins, G. (2022). *Introduction to clinical hypnosis: The basics and beyond.* Mountain Pine Publishing.

Elkins, G. & Olendzki, N. (2019). *Mindful hypnotherapy: The basics for clinical practice.* Springer Publishing Co.

Elkins, G., Barabasz, A., Council, J., & Spiegel, D. (2015). Advancing research and practice: The Revised APA Division 30 Definition of Hypnosis. *International Journal of Clinical and Experimental Hypnosis*, 63(1), 1–9. https://doi.org/10.1080/00207144.2014.961870

Chapter 2
How Does Hypnotherapy Work?

CAMERON ALLDREDGE
GARY ELKINS

As we discussed in the previous chapter, hypnosis is a natural state of consciousness involving focused attention and an increased ability for mental imagery and response to suggestions. Hypnotherapy is relaxing, enhances the mind-body connection, and allows for suggestions to be processed at both conscious and unconscious levels. A hypnotic induction is the process that serves to guide a person into a relaxed state of focused attention. In this state, there are changes in brain activity in which the conscious processing of information is lessened, the conscious mind is quieted, and there is a greater ability to process suggestions within the experiential system of our mind (a.k.a. the unconscious mind). In a state of hypnosis, a person becomes more open and receptive to positive ideas and suggestions. There are multiple components of hypnotherapy and modern science has provided some insight into how this process works.

Your Brain and Hypnosis

Your brain is an amazing and complex organ. It allows you to think, solve problems, interpret sensations, and experience emotions. It also operates in such a way that allows you to experience the state of consciousness that we refer to as *hypnosis*. To understand the brain mechanisms that underlie the power of hypnotherapy, it is helpful to consider the main brain networks that are involved. The three brain networks that are involved with the hypnotic state and response to hypnotic suggestions are: the Salience Network; the Executive Control Network; and the Default Mode Network. These brain regions are illustrated here:

Scientists have found that, in hypnosis, there is *increased* activity in the Salience Network (which is associated with selecting where to direct attention) and *decreased* activity in the Default Mode Network (which is associated with self-awareness and internal processing). These alterations lead to intense focused attention, vivid mental imagery, absorption, and unconscious processing of information. Simultaneously, activity in the Executive Control Network (which is associated with conscious effort) is *decreased* which allows for hypnotic suggestions to be experienced effortlessly. In other words, it doesn't feel like the experience requires much mental energy.

Harnessing the Relaxation Response

Hypnotherapy allows you to enter a deeply relaxed state of mind and body. During deep hypnotic relaxation, there are a number of physiological responses that tend to occur:

- heart rate decreases
- muscle tension is reduced
- respiration rate is slowed

- blood pressure decreases
- there is a sense of psychological peace and calmness

During hypnosis, there is often a sense of present-moment awareness (like mindfulness) and an ability to simply notice and allow feelings and images to occur. As a person becomes more deeply relaxed, there is also decreased activity in the part of the brain involved in effortful thinking and movement (the dorsal anterior cingulate cortex). Suggestions for relaxation are at the core of reducing stress, preparing for deep sleep, reducing pain, and responding to other hypnotherapeutic suggestions.

Increased Mind-Body Connection

There is a connection between the mind and the body. Our thoughts, conscious or unconscious, can have profound effects on our mood, emotional reactions, and physical responses. The mind-body connection is particularly mobilized when hypnotherapy is applied to health conditions such as menopausal hot flashes, pain management, irritable bowel syndrome, or sleep problems. In the brain, this may be reflected in increased activity between the dorsolateral prefrontal cortex (which plays a role in decision making and attention) and the insula (which plays a role in emotional integration and self-awareness).

Hypnotherapy is an *experiential therapy*; meaning that the hypnotic suggestions are processed at an unconscious level and experienced as if they are really happening. This also works through the mind-body connection. For example, if a hypnotic suggestion is given to experience a sour taste from eating a lemon, then the brain can respond by experiencing the imaginary lemon which leads to a *real* physical sensation (increased salivation). In hypnotherapy, we make use of this process to target symptoms, improve health, and empower individuals to use the mind-body connection to benefit their own wellbeing.

Increased Ability to Respond to Positive Ideas

Hypnotic suggestions are typically formulated in positive terms. This is because hypnotherapy tends to work best when the therapy focuses on what a person *wants* rather than what they *don't want*. Having someone talk about what they *don't want* is not helpful unless there's a greater emphasis on positive suggestions for what the person *does want* (e.g., peace, comfort, motivation, control). The mind tends to latch on to what is being suggested—even if the word "not" or "don't" comes before it. For example, there's a big difference in how our mind would respond to the suggestion, "*Don't* **get stressed** *when you're giving a presentation*" compared to, "*From now on, when you give a presentation, you feel calm and confident.*" Even though the desired outcome is basically the same, it is important to phrase the suggestions according to what is wanted so the mind doesn't get stuck on what is *un*wanted.

Within the hypnotic state, there is an increased sense of openness and acceptance of such positive hypnotic suggestions. It has been said that, in a hypnotic state, a person *becomes more open to positive ideas*. In brain imaging studies, this openness has been shown to be consistent with reduced activity between the dorsolateral prefrontal cortex and the posterior cingulate cortex. However, a person engaged in hypnotherapy may notice that they simply feel less critical and judgmental and have an increased ability to internalize suggestions for positive acceptance and change. This openness to positive suggestions and ideas is important in hypnotherapy for smoking cessation, improving sport performance, reducing feelings of anxiety and depression, stress management, and altering daily habits (e.g., eating, exercise, and other health-related behaviors).

Facilitated Insight

Hypnotherapy also works to facilitate insight into underlying dynamics and problems that may be contributing to self-defeating habits, behaviors, thoughts, or emotions. Adverse childhood events, past trauma, insecurities, and negative experiences may continue to have an impact on a person even if they have "dealt" with the event or have no conscious awareness of it. In a hypnotherapy session, it is possible to enter a deeply relaxed state in which conscious defenses are lessened. Within this state of consciousness, unconscious material can be more easily accessed and addressed. Such factors (e.g., trauma, fear, grief, feelings of inferiority, unhelpful beliefs, stresses, etc.) can underlie many self-defeating behaviors and feelings. Hypnotherapy can help a person to become more aware of the impact of such factors and to bring them into conscious awareness for processing. Additionally, hypnosis can help a person to become more aware of their thoughts, feelings, goals, and preferences. In this way, hypnotherapy has some similarities to mindfulness and cognitive-behavioral therapy. Increased self-awareness and insight can be very helpful in making positive changes as well as self-acceptance, empathy, and compassion.

Communication with the Unconscious Mind

Psychologists have long known that information (and suggestions) is processed at two different levels of consciousness. We call one of these levels the *conscious* (or rational) *mind*. The other we generally refer to as the *unconscious* (or experiential) *mind*. The *Adaptive Experiential Theory* of hypnosis highlights these two levels of consciousness and uses them to explain how hypnosis works. The theory proposes that the conscious mind uses logic, rational thinking, and critical reasoning to deal with problems; it processes information more analytically. This is very useful in many circumstances, but the conscious mind works more slowly and has its limitations regarding changes in feelings, behaviors, and physiology.

On the other hand, the unconscious mind is more *experiential* and processes information more quickly and holistically. The language of the unconscious mind (and therefore the language of hypnotherapy) relies more on the following:

- Mental imagery
- Metaphors
- Intuition
- Narratives
- Associative examples
- Emotion
- Experiences

It is understood that a hypnotic induction helps to facilitate a hypnotic state which gives us direct access to the unconscious mind. In essence, it helps shift a person's processing from rational to experiential. Hypnotherapy works by facilitating the opportunity and circumstances to have a real and influential *experience*. Rationally thinking and talking about a problem can be helpful, but we propose that true change follows experience.

Traditional psychotherapy approaches often consist of sessions centered around talking that involves education, problem-solving, strategizing, and processing. Then, the therapist sends patients on their way *hoping* that the talking will lead to a real experience outside of the session that solidifies what they discussed and eventually leads to long-lasting change. Hypnotherapy doesn't leave these crucial experiences up to chance, so the whole focus of hypnotherapy sessions is to have the experiences in the moment. In the field of psychotherapy, these trends are becoming increasingly apparent as more patients seek treatment that integrates mental imagery and profound experience in sessions.

Learning Self-Hypnosis

Hypnotherapy also works by teaching individuals how to practice self-hypnosis. This may involve listening to audio recordings for hypnotic inductions and positive therapeutic suggestions or learning how to enter the hypnotic state on their own. This can be very empowering as a person learns how to experience self-hypnosis in a way that is always accessible. Once learned and practiced, it can be used for stress management, pain reduction, performance enhancement, personal growth, and many other applications.

For example, self-hypnosis can be used to develop better coping skills in dealing with stressful situations. The person learns how to focus on their breathing, enter a deeply relaxed state, bring positive images to mind, and reinforce positive self-suggestions before returning to normal alertness. In fact, most hypnotherapy interventions include audio recordings for the practice of self-hypnosis to reinforce positive suggestions, develop coping skills, and prevent relapse after goals are achieved.

Summary

Hypnotherapy works through multiple components including the relaxation response, increased mind-body connection, increased ability to respond to positive ideas, more direct communication with the unconscious mind, increased access to insight, and learning self-hypnosis. Hypnotherapy uses the language of the unconscious mind such as mental imagery, metaphors, and emotion-based suggestions as well as direct suggestions. There are several brain areas and networks that are involved in experiencing the hypnotic state and hypnotic responses. Finally, it is helpful to consider that, in many ways, hypnotherapy works by facilitating the opportunity and circumstances to have a real and influential *experience* during sessions.

REFERENCES

Aleksandrowicz, J. W., Binder, M., & Urbanik, A. (2007). Hypnosis and analgesic suggestions in fMRI. *Archives of Psychiatry and Psychotherapy*, *9*(3), 25–33.

Alldredge, C., & Elkins, G. (2023). Adaptive experiential theory of hypnosis. *International Journal of Clinical and Experimental Hypnosis, 71*(3), 165–175.

Bensen, H. (1985). *Beyond the relaxation response.* Berkley.

Elkins, G. (2017). *Handbook of medical and psychological hypnosis: Foundations, applications, and professional issues.* Springer Publishing Inc.

Elkins, G. (2022). *Introduction to clinical hypnosis: The basics and beyond.* Mountain Pine Publishing.

Jiang, H., White, M. P., Greicius, M. D., Waelde, L. C., & Spiegel, D. (2017). Brain activity and functional connectivity associated with hypnosis. *Cerebral Cortex, 27*(8), 4083–4093. https://doi.org/10.1093/cercor/bhw220

McGeown, William J., Mazzoni, G., Venneri, A., & Kirsch, I. (2009). Hypnotic induction decreases anterior default mode activity. *Consciousness and Cognition, 18*(4), 848–855. https://doi.org/10.1016/j.concog.2009.09.001

Chapter 3
What Happens During a Hypnotherapy Session?

CAMERON ALLDREDGE

GARY ELKINS

Each hypnotherapy session is different depending on the goals of that particular session. The following case provides an example of what generally happens during hypnotherapy sessions with a therapist.

The Case of Amy and Her Hypnotherapy Sessions

Amy sat anxiously in the waiting room of Dr. Anderson's office. She was a 38-year-old woman with trauma in her past who recently began experiencing sleep problems. She went to a few therapy sessions after her traumatic incident in her early 20s but dropped out when she felt she was too busy to keep meeting with her therapist. After discussing her struggles with a co-worker, she was encouraged to reach out to Dr. Anderson's office and schedule an appointment with him. Her co-worker told her that Dr. Anderson was a psychologist trained in hypnotherapy and used hypnosis with his patients. Amy didn't know much about hypnosis other than what she had seen in movies and a stage hypnosis show she saw in college.

Dr. Anderson entered the waiting room and invited Amy by name to follow him to his office. They entered the comfortably lit room and Dr.

Anderson gestured to Amy to sit down in the cozy recliner opposite of his own chair. The room contained a bookshelf, a desk, and some calming art hanging on the walls. Dr. Anderson smiled as he told Amy he was happy she had reached out to him and that he looked forward to getting to know her better so he could determine how he might be able to help her.

Over the next thirty minutes, Amy started to feel more relaxed and unguarded as Dr. Anderson asked her questions about her childhood, family, education, work, relationships, and interests. He seemed genuinely interested in what she had to say and allowed her to answer his questions with as much detail as she wanted. He asked helpful follow-up questions that sparked deeper reflection, and she felt herself opening up about things that she usually didn't talk about.

"So, the big question I have for you is: what do you hope to gain from our sessions together?" asked Dr. Anderson.

Amy thought for a moment and answered, tentatively, "I know I need to figure out my sleep, and it would probably be good for me to address some of the trauma I've experienced. I don't think I ever completely dealt with it."

The two spoke in depth about these issues and began to discuss the next steps of treatment. Amy told Dr. Anderson she was interested in trying hypnosis, but she wanted to learn more about it first. Dr. Anderson met her hesitation with compassionate understanding and asked what she knew about hypnosis.

"Well," Amy responded, "I've had some friends try hypnotherapy and it seems to have really helped them. They said it was really relaxing and helped them make important changes in their life. I was surprised to learn that they could remember what happened during the hypnosis and they didn't feel a loss of control."

Dr. Anderson nodded encouragingly and gathered more detailed information about Amy's perceptions of hypnosis. He then spent some time explaining what hypnosis is, what it can feel like, what to expect, and how it can help. He emphasized the importance of Amy practicing on her own in between their sessions. This information helped Amy feel at ease and hopeful that hypnosis could help her. They then discussed what specific changes Amy wanted to achieve and what approaches might be

Chapter 3: What Happens During a Hypnotherapy Session?

the most appropriate. Together, they decided to start with improving her sleep and then shift to focus on her trauma.

"Let's go ahead and try some hypnosis, if that sounds alright with you." Dr. Anderson suggested calmly.

Amy nodded in agreement and shifted comfortably in the recliner. Dr. Anderson instructed Amy to recline her chair back to a relaxing position and asked her to stare at a spot on the ceiling above her. As she fixed her gaze on the ceiling, Dr. Anderson asked her to slow down her breathing and focus on relaxing her body. After about one minute, he instructed her to close her eyes and provided helpful suggestions for Amy to relax various parts of her body and to feel safe, peaceful, and at ease.

Soon, Amy felt like her body was weightless and she was floating. Her mind was focused intently on being in a pleasant place and it really felt like she was there. In Amy's mind, she was sitting on the beach her family loved to visit. She felt the warmth of the sun, the gentle breeze, and the soft sand. She could see the beautiful vista and the reflection of sunlight shimmering on the water's surface. She could smell the ocean air and hear the sound of the waves. It was so peaceful. She found that she could hear what Dr. Anderson was saying but it faded in and out of importance to her. Her mind and body felt completely calm and relaxed.

With hypnotic suggestions from Dr. Anderson, Amy was guided through several positive experiences related to improved sleep. She experienced what it would be like to get ready for bed and then fall asleep quickly and easily. She experienced what it would be like to wake up feeling well-rested, refreshed, and energized. She also experienced specific ways her life might be improved if she were to consistently get good sleep. As she had all these experiences, she noticed she began to feel more and more hopeful that her sleeping could improve. It not only seemed possible, but like she personally possessed the ability to have good sleep. This led to a feeling of motivation to engage in better sleep hygiene and to have positive expectations about her sleep.

After what seemed like only a few minutes since she closed her eyes, Dr. Anderson began to tell Amy that she would soon open her eyes feeling alert and rejuvenated. When her eyes opened, she sat up slowly and stretched. She felt like she had just woken up from a restful nap but felt calmly alert. She could remember everything she had seen, heard, and experienced during the hypnosis. They sat in brief silence as she explored the positive and motivating feelings that now filled her mind and body.

Before leaving Dr. Anderson's office, they discussed her experience and made concrete plans for positive changes she could start to make during the week. They scheduled their next session for the following week and Amy left feeling hopeful and determined. Over the next few days, she reflected on her experience often and allowed it to guide a new way of living. During quiet times of the day, she sat down in her favorite chair, closed her eyes, relaxed her body, and rehearsed the experiences she had in Dr. Anderson's office. Her sleep began to improve, and she noticed she could function better throughout the day because she felt well-rested.

Over the next couple of months, Amy returned to Dr. Anderson's office each week for additional sessions. The sessions usually started with a review of Amy's progress since their last session and the effects she noticed in her day-to-day life. This was followed by collaborative planning on what they should focus on that day. Then, Dr. Anderson would invite Amy to get into a comfortable position, close her eyes, and would guide her into a mental and physical state of peaceful relaxation. During the relaxation, Amy would be provided with suggestions for a variety of helpful experiences. Before the end of each session, Dr. Anderson would invite Amy to open her eyes and feel alert. After opening her eyes and sitting up, Amy would usually stretch with a smile, and they would discuss her experience. Once she was satisfied with her improved sleeping habits, they shifted their focus to addressing her past trauma. After about six sessions, they both decided that weekly sessions were no longer necessary, and Amy could check in every month or so if it seemed helpful.

Analysis of Amy's Experience

This story of Amy illustrates a somewhat typical course of hypnotherapy. While many elements of treatment will depend on the clinicians' personal approach, most professionals follow a similar pattern. The initial or "intake" session tends to focus on gathering a lot of background information, setting overarching goals for treatment, and discussing hypnosis as a treatment option. If the plan is to use hypnosis over the span of multiple sessions, most sessions begin with an update about how things are going followed by a determination of goals for the session. After that, the clinician usually facilitates some sort of *hypnotic induction* which typically involves calming suggestions for mental and physical relaxation. As treatment progresses, the induction tends to get shorter and more effective because the mind and body are already familiar with the state of hypnosis and it's easier to enter into it.

Following the induction, clinicians typically provide suggestions for certain experiences that correlate with the predetermined goals. In the chapters that follow, you will get a good sense of what these suggestions might look like for various issues. *Posthypnotic suggestions* are also common during this phase which may involve sensations, thoughts, or behaviors that will happen when a person is out of hypnosis living their normal, day-to-day life.

Once all the suggestions have been given (and usually repeated for reinforcement), the clinician will *re-alert* the person back to normal consciousness. Many clinicians use counting as a method for this. For example, a clinician might say "On the count of five, you can open your eyes and return to regular conscious alertness." Once a person is fully alert and re-oriented, their experiences are discussed, and plans are made for positive changes. Clinicians often assign "homework" to be completed between sessions and provide encouragement for patients to practice self-hypnosis at home. They may provide audio recordings of hypnosis or refer them to a smartphone app to help with this practice.

We'd like to point out that one of the major differences between hypnosis and other approaches (such as mindfulness or meditation) is that hypnotherapy sessions are always guided by a specific goal. Whatever the goal happens to be, that is what shapes the experience and everything else is crafted around it. The hypnotic suggestions are all aimed at creating a powerful experience that helps lead to the realization of that goal. Understandably, goals seem much more achievable after you've already experienced yourself achieving them. That is why specific goals are so crucial in hypnotherapy sessions.

Summary

The basic format for most hypnotherapy sessions involves:

1. Gather information and/or review progress
2. Set goals for the session
3. Hypnotic induction
4. Hypnotic suggestions
5. Re-alert
6. Debrief
7. Make plans

Combined with a competent professional and a trusting relationship, this format can be used and adapted to treat a variety of issues. When we (CA and GE) see clients, this is the process we typically follow.

REFERENCES

Elkins, G. (2014). *Hypnotic relaxation therapy: Principles and applications.* Springer Publishing Co.

Elkins, G. (2022). *Introduction to clinical hypnosis: The basics and beyond.* Mountain Pine Publishing.

Milling, L. S. (2023). *Evidence-based practice in clinical hypnosis.* American Psychological Association.

Chapter 4
Is Hypnosis Safe?

Skyla Renner-Wilms
Gary Elkins

Hypnosis is a natural state of consciousness that most people experience as pleasant, safe, and empowering. To have an understanding of the safety of hypnosis, consider the definition, hypnosis is *a state of consciousness involving focused attention and reduced peripheral awareness, characterized by an enhanced capacity for response to suggestion.* Just like the definition outlines, hypnosis involves being completely absorbed in an experience with minimal analytic interference. In this state, hypnotic suggestions are perceived, and we simply have the increased capacity to respond to these new circumstances as if they are actually happening. Like in dreaming, we can nonjudgmentally accept the experience and hypnotic suggestions as they occur. The experience in hypnosis temporarily becomes our reality.

During a hypnotic induction, individuals are usually guided to focus their attention, close their eyes, become deeply relaxed, and be open to mental imagery, metaphors, and suggestions. For example, a hypnotic induction might include suggestions such as:

> *"All hypnotic inductions begin with a focus of attention, and for our purposes today…you can settle into the cushions of the chair…and when you are ready to enter a hypnotic state…closing your eyes…as the eyelids close…focusing your attention on your breathing…notice the coolness of the air as you breathe in…and*

the feeling of letting go…as you breathe out…soon becoming more and more relaxed…Each breath of air can take you into a deeper hypnotic state…more relaxed…where you can accomplish the things you wish to accomplish today."

The Safe Use of Hypnosis

As illustrated in this example, hypnotherapy is an experiential therapy. It is something you do and experience in your own way. It also involves "letting go" of conscious, critical thinking and being open to the therapeutic suggestions that are given. Therefore, there are several guidelines for safety in hypnosis sessions. These include:

- Do not listen to a hypnosis session when you are driving a car or engaging in any activity that requires your attention to things going on around you.
- You should practice hypnosis when you are in a place or room where you will not be distracted, interrupted, or disturbed.
- You should set aside sufficient time for self-hypnosis (usually about 20–30 minutes).
- You should be in a place where you can close your eyes and feel safe.
- You should either sit in a comfortable position or lie down with good support for your head, neck, and shoulders.

With these conditions, hypnosis is generally considered to be safe, with few or no negative effects. It is always possible that a person might have a memory that brings some anxiety or a negative reaction to some mental imagery (for example, some people like the mental imagery of a beach or ocean and some do not).

Hypnosis is commonly experienced as empowering. As a personal experiment, go ahead and think of a change in your life that you wish you could have. Perhaps you wish that you had greater peace, more control, better focus, improved self-image, or healthier habits. Now, consider how much more likely it would be for that change to occur if you had already experienced what it would be like. Suddenly, it seems a lot more achievable. You have a positive expectation that change will occur and guide your actions to make it happen. It's as if you knew you couldn't fail because you already knew it could happen!

Consulting the Science

In clinical studies, hypnosis has been shown to be safe and some studies have specifically examined adverse events during hypnotherapy. For example, one systematic review on hypnotherapy for sleep found that participants who received hypnosis treatment reported improved sleep and there was no evidence that hypnosis was associated with adverse events. In research, an *adverse event* is defined as any undesirable experience or side effect that participants may encounter during a study. Similarly, another systematic review specifically looked at the safety of hypnosis in medical randomized controlled trials (RCTs). This study found that participants who received hypnotherapy reported no more adverse events than those who did not receive hypnotherapy. These scientific studies indicate that adverse events rarely occur during hypnosis and individuals undergoing hypnotherapy have no more risk of experiencing negative side effects than someone who did not receive hypnotherapy at all.

    Furthermore, a comprehensive meta-analysis involving 3,632 patients concluded that hypnosis is a safe and effective alternative to using medications for pain relief. Another review examined 49 meta-analyses that looked at the use of hypnosis for mental and physical health problems. This review found that participants experienced no serious adverse events. In the remaining studies, any reported adverse events were deemed minimal.

Clinical Perspective

A large international survey involving nearly 700 hypnosis practitioners provided insights into how hypnosis is utilized in clinical settings and its effectiveness for various applications. When asked about the adverse effects of hypnosis, nearly half of the clinicians (44.7%) reported that *none* of their clients had ever experienced any side effects from hypnosis. The clinicians who did report ever observing any adverse events stated this occurred in only 1% to 5% of their clients. When any adverse events were reported, they were transient, typically lasting no more than a few minutes. In short, clinicians report that their clients generally do not experience any adverse side effects during hypnotherapy, and any experienced side effects lasted only for a few minutes (such as a feeling of discomfort).

This suggests that hypnotherapy is very safe when delivered by a trained therapist. In fact, it may have fewer side effects than other therapies such as psychotherapy or medications. For example, studies of cognitive-behavioral therapy (CBT) generally report that about 10% of participants have some adverse/unwanted effects. In a systematic review of CBT, 10% of participants in CBT reported at least one adverse event and 17% dropped out. In another study of CBT, 17% reported at least one adverse event, 0–10% met criteria for overall symptom deterioration. Therefore, the evidence suggests that hypnotherapy may be safer than other widely used therapies such as CBT.

Summary

Hypnotherapy is widely recognized to be safe and effective for many concerns. Research indicates that most individuals who undergo hypnosis experience no treatment-related adverse effects. Compared to other psychological interventions or medications, hypnosis has fewer side effects and risks. In the rare instances where adverse events occur during hypnotherapy, they may include brief emotional reactions and mild physical discomfort. If you have any concerns about these potential effects, please consult your doctor before hypnotherapy. Hypnosis can be practiced through listening to audio recordings, self-hypnosis, or working with a therapist. Some guidelines for safely practicing hypnosis include being in an environment where you will not be disturbed and able to become fully absorbed in the experience.

REFERENCES

Axelsson, E., & Hedman-Lagerlöf, E. (2023). Unwanted outcomes in cognitive behavior therapy for pathological health anxiety: A systematic review and a secondary original study of two randomized controlled trials. *Expert Review of Pharmacoeconomics & Outcomes Research*, *23*(9), 1001–1015. https://doi.org/10.1080/14737167.2023.2250915

Chamine, I., Atchley, R., & Oken, B. S. (2018). Hypnosis intervention effects on sleep outcomes: A systematic review. *Journal of Clinical Sleep Medicine, 14*(2), 271–283. https://doi.org/10.5664/jcsm.6952

Häuser, W., Hagl, M., Schmierer, A., & Hansen, E. (2016). The efficacy, safety and applications of medical hypnosis. *Deutsches Arzteblatt International*, *113*(17), 289–296. https://doi.org/10.3238/arztebl.2016.0289

Palsson, O. S., Kekecs, Z., De Benedittis, G., Moss, D., Elkins, G. R., Terhune, D. B., Varga, K., Shenefelt, P. D., Whorwell, P. J. (2023). Current practices, experiences, and views in clinical hypnosis: Findings of an international survey. *International Journal of Clinical and Experimental Hypnosis*, *71*(2), 92–114. https://doi.org/10.1080/00207144.2023.2183862

Rosendahl, J., Alldredge, C. T., & Haddenhorst, A. (2024). Meta-analytic evidence on the efficacy of hypnosis for mental and somatic health issues: A 20-year perspective. *Frontiers in Psychology*, *14*, 1330238. https://doi.org/10.3389/fpsyg.2023.1330238

Thompson, T., Terhune, D. B., Oram, C., Sharangparni, J., Rouf, R., Solmi, M., Veronese, N., & Stubbs, B. (2019). The effectiveness of hypnosis for pain relief: A systematic review and meta-analysis of 85 controlled experimental trials. *Neuroscience and Biobehavioral Reviews*, *99*, 298–310. https://doi.org/10.1016/j.neubiorev.2019.02.013

Chapter 5
How Popular Is Hypnotherapy?

VANESSA MUÑIZ
CHRIS CORLETT
GARY ELKINS

As you will read later in the book, research has shown that hypnotherapy has a wide range of applications such as smoking cessation, irritable bowel syndrome, pain management, menopausal symptoms such as hot flashes, stress, and sleep improvement. The quality of research has greatly improved over the past 30 years and more people are seeking and using hypnosis through hypnotherapy apps, working with health care providers, and practicing self-hypnosis on their own. Several surveys of the adult population in the United States have provided a clear understanding that clinical hypnosis is generally seen very positively and is well received. Many people want more information about hypnosis. Further, it is practiced by a significant number of clinicians globally, and its use spans a variety of therapeutic contexts.

For instance, a research survey focusing on what works and doesn't work for smoking cessation interviewed 1,175 individuals to gauge what smoking cessation techniques are used the most often and what is the perceived efficacy of these treatments. In this large survey, hypnosis was found to be among the most highly rated treatments (13% reported use), with 40% of the participants reporting they'd be interested in trying it in the future. Agreeing with the participants' high preference, hypnosis was one of the two most tested interventions in randomized-controlled trials and provided moderate to high efficacy. (For more information on hypnosis for smoking cessation, see Chapter 8).

Research on the popularity of clinical hypnosis for numerous other conditions has shown that there is a consistent, promising openness and positive attitude toward hypnotherapy in individuals with and without prior exposure to hypnosis! In fact, most studies focusing on the attitudes and views towards hypnosis show that there is a general positive attitude, and a high percentage of the population share that they would use hypnotherapy if offered by a health care provider.

Hypnotherapy Use Among Health Care Practitioners

Now that we have discussed the popularity of hypnotherapy among the general population, we also want to consider the interest in hypnotherapy among physicians, psychologists, and health-care providers. Clinical hypnosis is a globally available intervention, with over 30 countries having practicing professionals. In a recent international survey that included over 650 hypnosis practitioners, clinical hypnosis was found to be most commonly used by licensed clinical psychologists (42.7%), although physicians, social workers, dentists, and nurses were also well-represented.

Before diving deeper into the most popular clinical applications of hypnotherapy, it is important to note that, although clinical hypnosis is defined as *hypnotherapy* by Division 30 of the American Psychological Association and incorporated into psychotherapeutic interventions, such as cognitive behavioral therapy, it is also highly effective in boosting benefits across diverse therapies and for many clinical conditions.

For example, a recent meta-analysis found that when clinical hypnosis was combined with cognitive behavioral therapy (CBT) for depression and pain, treatment efficacy was greater than when CBT was used alone. Similarly, in another meta-analysis, hypnotherapy for the reduction of anxiety was more effective when combined with other psychotherapeutic interventions than when it was used alone.

Most Popular Applications of Hypnosis

In a 2019 survey of 1,000 adults, it was found that almost 90% of respondents had a positive or neutral view of clinical hypnosis. Forty-seven percent of respondents said they thought hypnosis was effective for treating medical problems, almost 60% think it is useful for treating emotional problems, and 60% think it is useful for fixing bad habits. Finally, 55% reported that they probably or definitely would consider seeking hypnosis treatment if they had a physical or psychological health problem known to be improved by hypnosis.

There are a number of cases for which hypnosis is particularly effective. A 2023 international survey of hypnosis practitioners noted that stress reduction, preparation for surgery, wellbeing and self-esteem enhancement, anxiety treatment, improvement of mindfulness, and labor and childbirth applications were rated as effective uses of hypnosis by over 70% of the 691 participants in the study. Additionally, over 60% of hypnotherapists reported hypnosis as an effective technique for post-traumatic stress disorder, facilitating personal insight, panic disorder, phobias, and reducing pain during medical procedures. Finally, as mentioned in the previous chapter, hypnosis is generally considered to be very safe. In that same survey, 44% of the clinicians surveyed have never encountered hypnosis-associated adverse events. For those clinicians that did, they estimated the adverse events as having occurred in only 1% of their clients, didn't last long, and were rarely serious. Some examples of the most common side include feelings of drowsiness, emotional upset, and minor disorientation and headaches (the same you would get from taking a lengthy nap).

As well, hypnosis is one of only two nonpharmacological treatments recommended for hot flashes by the North American Menopause Society with level one status, indicating good, reliable scientific evidence. In fact, in a recent scoping review, Muñiz and colleagues found that while cognitive behavioral therapy can help reduce daily interference, bother, or self-reported perception of problematic hot flashes, it did not actually reduce hot flashes. Hypnosis, on the other hand, demonstrated clinically significant efficacy to treat and reduce hot flashes in both frequency and severity across all of its clinical trials.

As you can see, hypnosis can be an effective treatment for a wide range of conditions, preparing for or coping with medical or dental procedures, and even enhancement of daily life through mindfulness or personal insight. Hypnosis can also be used in any of these instances as an alternative treatment for people who don't want to use pharmaceutical drugs, don't respond normally to anesthesia, or experience discomfort with traditional medical procedures. If this is the case, then why don't more people use hypnosis?

Why Isn't Hypnotherapy Even More Widely Used?

While there is great interest in hypnotherapy, many people are uncertain about how to best access hypnotherapy apps or find a practitioner. Although hypnotherapy is usually reported to be a highly pleasant and effective treatment by most patients, there are still barriers to accessing hypnotherapy in clinical settings. Clinical hypnosis would be used more if there were more hypnotherapists, better education about hypnosis, and increased access to scholarly research on hypnotherapy.

It is generally the case that increased understanding leads to greater engagement. Evidence suggests that most adults hold positive or neutral views of hypnosis and recognize its basis of good scientific evidence. Practical barriers may also contribute to underutilization, particularly among older adults who may face additional challenges in accessing care. Limited availability of trained clinicians and a lack of widespread awareness about alternative delivery methods, such as audiotapes or smartphone apps, further impede access.

How Easily Can Hypnotherapy be Accessed?

Practical barriers play a role in accessing hypnotherapy for stress, smoking cessation, sleep, mindfulness, and symptom management. This can partly be addressed as more individuals are trained in hypnotherapy. Another emerging way to increase easy access is through evidence-based hypnotherapy apps such as those provided by Mindset Health. In the chapters of this book, you will be able to gain more knowledge and dive more in-depth on the common clinical applications for which most people seek hypnotherapy that were mentioned above. Additionally, Chapter 24 (Beginning Hypnotherapy and Additional Resources) provides information on how to find a hypnotherapist and digital hypnotherapy apps that provide evidence-based interventions with trained, certified consultants.

Summary

Hypnosis has a wide range of applications. In multiple surveys, it has been shown that most people have a relatively high opinion of hypnosis and what it may be able to do for them, even when compared to other treatments. Over 30 countries have professional clinical hypnosis practitioners. However, hypnosis can still be difficult to access for many. Barriers to access could be reduced if there were more hypnotherapists, better education about hypnosis, and improved access to scholarly research on hypnotherapy. This is beginning to change, however. There are now a number of relatively affordable hypnosis-focused smart phone applications that can be used for general use or clinical issues. We hope you can take advantage of these, and that the hypnosis community continues to address issues of ready and affordable access.

REFERENCES

Dwight-Johnson, M., Sherbourne, C. D., Liao, D., & Wells, K. B. (2000). Treatment preferences among depressed primary care patients. *Journal of General Internal Medicine, 15*(8), 527–534. https://doi.org/10.1046/j.1525-1497.2000.08035.x

Green, J. P., Laurence, J.-R., & Lynn, S. J. (2014). Hypnosis and psychotherapy: From Mesmer to mindfulness. *Psychology of Consciousness: Theory, Research, and Practice, 1*(2), 199–212. https://doi.org/10.1037/cns0000015

Green, J., Page, R., Rasekhy, R., Johnson, L., & Bernhardt, S. (2006). Cultural views and attitudes about hypnosis: A survey of college students across four countries. *International Journal of Clinical and Experimental Hypnosis, 54*(3), 263–280. https://doi.org/10.1080/00207140600689439

Krouwel, M., Jolly, K., & Greenfield, S. (2017). What the public think about hypnosis and hypnotherapy: A narrative review of literature covering opinions and attitudes of the general public 1996–2016. *Complementary Therapies in Medicine, 32,* 75–84. https://doi.org/10.1016/j.ctim.2017.04.002

Lavingia, R., Jones, K., & Asghar-Ali, A. (2020). A systematic review of barriers faced by older adults in seeking and accessing mental health care. *Journal of Psychiatric Practice, 26*(5), 367–382. https://doi.org/10.1097/PRA.0000000000000491

Lynn, S. J., Kirsch, I., Terhune, D. B., & Green, J. P. (2020). Myths and misconceptions about hypnosis and suggestion: Separating fact and fiction. *Applied Cognitive Psychology, 34*(6), 1253–1264. https://doi.org/10.1002/acp.3730

Moss, D. (2020). Paradigms in integrative medicine and the place of clinical hypnosis. *OBM Integrative and Complementary Medicine, 5*(1), 1007. https://doi.org/10.21926/obm.icm.2001007

Muñiz V., Padilla V. J., Alldredge C. T., Elkins G. (in press). Clinical Hypnosis and Cognitive Behavioral Therapy for Hot Flashes: A Scoping Review. *Women's Health Reports.*

Palsson, O. S., Kekecs, Z., De Benedittis, G., Moss, D., Elkins, G. R., Terhune, D. B., Varga, K., Shenefelt, P. D., & Whorwell, P. J. (2023). Current practices, experiences, and views in clinical hypnosis: Findings of an international survey. *International Journal of Clinical and Experimental Hypnosis, 71*(2), 92–114. https://doi.org/10.1080/00207144.2023.2183862

Palsson, O., Twist, S., & Walker, M. (2019). A national survey of clinical hypnosis views and experiences of the adult population in the United States. *International Journal of Clinical and Experimental Hypnosis, 67*(4), 428–448. https://doi.org./10.1080/00207144.2019.1649538

Pepin, R., Segal, D. L., & Coolidge, F. L. (2009). Intrinsic and extrinsic barriers to mental health care among community-dwelling younger and older adults. *Aging & Mental Health, 13*(5), 769–777. https://doi.org/10.1080/13607860902918231

Ramondo, N., Gignac, G. E., Pestell, C. F., & Byrne, S. M. (2021). Clinical hypnosis as an adjunct to cognitive behavior therapy: An updated meta-analysis. *International Journal of Clinical and Experimental Hypnosis, 69*(2), 169–202. https://doi.org/10.1080/00207144.2021.1877549

Sood, A., Ebbert, J. O., Sood, R., & Stevens, S. R. (2006). Complementary treatments for tobacco cessation: A survey. *Nicotine & Tobacco Research, 8*(6), 767–771. https://doi.org/10.1080/14622200601004109

Valentine, K. E., Milling, L. S., Clark, L. J., & Moriarty, C. L. (2019). The efficacy of hypnosis as a treatment for anxiety: A meta-analysis. *International Journal of Clinical and Experimental Hypnosis, 67*(3), 336–363. https://doi.org/10.1080/00207144.2019.1613863

Chapter 6
Hypnotherapy: What the Science Says

KATIE SEIDENBERG
KATHERINE SCHEFFRAHN
CAMERON ALLDREDGE

The field of clinical hypnosis research is well-established, thriving, and expansive. While hypnotherapy has recently become more popular across the world, the scientific study of hypnosis itself has its roots in the 18th century. In this chapter, we will examine well-established areas of the hypnosis research field, developing areas of the field, and where people can find more research.

The Current State of Hypnosis Research

Today, a quick search on *PubMed* generates over 16,000 peer-reviewed articles on clinical hypnosis, over 1,400 of which were published in the past five years. With the first articles on hypnosis being published in the 1940s, hypnosis has a long history of scientific examination. While there are a variety of topics researched in the realm of hypnosis, most current research is focused on studying how hypnotherapy can be used to treat mental and physical issues.

The effectiveness of hypnotic interventions is well-documented across various research areas. For instance, hypnosis has a long history of use in pain management, dating back to the early 19th century when effective pain treatments were scarce. Contemporary research supports its efficacy, with a 2019 systematic review of 85 studies finding that clinical hypnosis can significantly alleviate pain in most people and serve as a safe alternative to pharmaceutical interventions. Similarly, treating stress and anxiety using clinical hypnosis has been studied extensively. A recent meta-analysis of 17 trials found that hypnotherapy reduced anxiety in individuals receiving hypnotic interventions by approximately 79% more than those in control conditions. Furthermore, clinical hypnosis has been widely investigated over the years for its efficacy in promoting health behavior changes. Specifically, studies have shown it to be an effective intervention for smoking cessation and weight loss.

A recent umbrella review published in 2024 synthesized the findings from 49 meta-analyses, which included a total of 261 distinct, randomized controlled trials investigating clinical hypnosis. This review assessed the efficacy of hypnotic interventions for symptom management in both emerging and well-established areas of clinical hypnosis research. These included medical procedures, labor and childbirth, pain, cancer, smoking cessation, irritable bowel syndrome, obesity, and various other issues. The review found that more than half of the studies reported at least a medium effect size, indicating that hypnotic interventions produce meaningful improvements in the outcomes of these conditions. While these results highlight the value of clinical hypnosis, it is important to note that experts emphasize that hypnosis often yields the best outcomes when combined with another evidence-based intervention (e.g., medication, psychotherapy, etc.) rather than being the sole treatment.

One current focus is the delivery of hypnotherapy through remote and digital means. The mobile health industry is expanding rapidly, as more and more people use virtual methods (e.g., apps, telehealth) to access healthcare. Clinical hypnosis is a great candidate to maximize this shift since effective hypnotherapy can be experienced through audio recordings. New research in this area is encouraging, with important implications for the field of hypnotherapy. For example, effective virtual delivery can make clinical hypnosis more cost-effective and boost its availability among people who would otherwise have limited access. An interesting area of this research examines the benefit of increased flexibility, which allows individuals to use hypnotherapy in the moments they are experiencing symptoms. Because of these benefits, much of the active hypnosis research is exploring digitally delivered hypnotherapy.

Researched Uses for Hypnotherapy

Clinical hypnosis has been examined for the treatment of many different problems. Much of the well-researched uses are included in later chapters of this book, but we do not exhaustively cover all areas of hypnotherapy research. Some of the uses with the strongest evidence are:

- Pain management: Arguably, one of the most researched areas of clinical hypnosis is its use to significantly reduce pain intensity and improve overall functioning for people who experience chronic pain (read more in Chapter 16).
- Anxiety and stress reduction: Research has found that clinical hypnosis is particularly apt for increasing sensations of peace and relaxation both physically and mentally which can combat thoughts and feelings of stress and worry (read more in Chapters 13 and 15).
- Hot flashes/menopausal symptoms: Extensive research has found clinical hypnosis to be the only non-drug method for reducing the frequency and severity of post-menopausal hot flashes (read more in Chapter 9).
- Sleep: Studies have found that hypnosis can help people fall asleep quicker, stay asleep throughout the night, and sleep more deeply (read more in Chapter 10).

- Irritable bowel syndrome (IBS): Many studies have found hypnotherapy helps significantly reduce IBS-related symptoms such as pain and discomfort and can help normalize bowel movements (read more in Chapter 12).
- Smoking cessation: This classic use of hypnotherapy has been examined by multiple researchers, and many findings suggest that clinical hypnosis can effectively help individuals stop or reduce smoking (read more in Chapter 8).
- Coping with medical and dental procedures: This is another area where some of the best hypnotherapy results are found, as hypnosis has been shown to reduce fear and anxiety, reduce pain, and enhance recovery (read more in Chapter 20).
- Phobias: Research suggests that hypnosis can act as a powerful tool for exposure-based therapies, which can be used to treat a wide variety of fears and phobias (read more in Chapter 14).
- Posttraumatic stress disorder (PTSD): Hypnotherapy has been shown to help with reframing traumatic events, decreasing reactions to external triggers, and increasing one's sense of safety (read more in Chapter 11).
- Weight management: Past research has found clinical hypnosis to alter food cravings and help individuals start and maintain habits related to a healthy lifestyle (read more in Chapter 18).

Emerging Areas of Research

One major area of interest in ongoing hypnosis research is looking at "moderators of efficacy," which means examining what specific hypnosis techniques work best, whom they work best for, and in which circumstances. Along these lines, there seems to be promising indications that children and adolescents have higher hypnotizability compared to adults on average; so, new research is focusing on how hypnosis could specifically benefit young people.

There are many areas of interest in clinical hypnosis where more research is needed, or new research is being conducted. These areas include eating disorders, lucid dreaming, allergies, Parkinson's disease, warts, asthma, dissociative disorders, bereavement, conversion disorder, enuresis, and many more. Because so much of human health and wellbeing is influenced by the mind-body connection, hypnotherapy has the potential to serve as a helpful treatment for many different concerns. That is why it is so important for researchers to thoroughly investigate and identify the research areas where scientific approaches yield the most sound and compelling evidence on hypnotherapy.

Where Can I Find More Hypnosis Research?

As the scientific study of hypnosis continues to grow, the field is propelled by professional organizations that support researchers and clinicians. If you wish to explore the science of hypnosis further after reading this book, there are a few places you can look. The American Society of Clinical Hypnosis (ASCH), the Society for Clinical and Experimental Hypnosis (SCEH), and Division 30 of the American Psychological Association (APA) are organizations that host professional conferences, workshops, and collaboration opportunities to expand the use and scientific inquiry of clinical hypnosis. There are also two scientific journals devoted entirely to publishing hypnosis research: the American Journal of Clinical Hypnosis (AJCH) and the International Journal of Clinical and Experimental Hypnosis (IJCEH) which is the premiere journal for hypnosis research. Valuable contributions to the field of hypnosis research occur around the world, with a number of laboratories focused on hypnosis and its clinical applications at institutions such as Stanford University, Eötvös Loránd University in Hungary, University of Washington School of Medicine, and Baylor

University, just to name a few. All these laboratories involve professors, research faculty, post-doctoral fellows, graduate student researchers, and undergraduate research assistants who work together to research hypnosis and hypnotherapy.

Summary

The field of hypnosis research is not a new one, with an extensive history of rigorous experimentation and exploration into how hypnotherapy may benefit different medical conditions and increase people's wellbeing. Thousands of research studies on hypnosis inform how clinicians may apply the intervention, and new research is ongoing. With laboratories across the world and journals publishing peer-reviewed hypnosis research, the field continues to expand and improve our understanding of hypnotherapy. This book is unique as each chapter will highlight what the science says and provide a broad overview of how hypnotherapy can help.

REFERENCES

Bicego, A., Rousseaux, F., Faymonville, M.-E., Nyssen, A.-S., & Vanhaudenhuyse, A. (2021). Neurophysiology of hypnosis in chronic pain: A review of recent literature. *American Journal of Clinical Hypnosis, 64*(1), 62–80. https://doi.org/10.1080/00029157.2020.1869517

Chaves, J. F., & Dworkin, S. F. (1997). Hypnotic control of pain: Historical perspectives and future prospects. *International Journal of Clinical and Experimental Hypnosis, 45*(4), 356–376. https://doi.org/10.1080/00207149708416138

Elkins, G. (2024). Clinical hypnosis intervention for improving sleep quality: Emerging research and future directions. *International Journal of Clinical and Experimental Hypnosis, 72*(2), 91–93. https://doi.org/10.1080/00207144.2024.2321103

Elkins, G. R. (2014). *Hypnotic relaxation therapy: Principles and applications.* Springer Pub. Co.

Elkins, G. R., Barabasz, A. F., Council, J. R., & Spiegel, D. (2015). Advancing research and practice: The revised APA Division 30 definition of hypnosis. *International Journal of Clinical and Experimental Hypnosis*, *63*(1), 1–9. https://doi.org/10.1080/00207144.2014.961870

Kekecs, Z., Bowers, J., Johnson, A., Kendrick, C., & Elkins, G. (2016). The Elkins Hypnotizability Scale: Assessment of reliability and validity. *International Journal of Clinical and Experimental Hypnosis*, *64*(3), 285–304. https://doi.org/10.1080/00207144.2016.1171089

Paul, R. D. (Ed.). (2021). *The Wiley Encyclopedia of Health Psychology* (First edition). Wiley-Blackwell.

Rosendahl, J., Alldredge, C. T., & Haddenhorst, A. (2024). Meta-analytic evidence on the efficacy of hypnosis for mental and somatic health issues: A 20-year perspective. *Frontiers in Psychology*, *14*. https://doi.org/10.3389/fpsyg.2023.1330238

Thompson, T., Terhune, D. B., Oram, C., Sharangparni, J., Rouf, R., Solmi, M., Veronese, N., & Stubbs, B. (2019). The effectiveness of hypnosis for pain relief: A systematic review and meta-analysis of 85 controlled experimental trials. *Neuroscience and Biobehavioral Reviews*, *99*, 298–310. Scopus. https://doi.org/10.1016/j.neubiorev.2019.02.013

Valentine, K. E., Milling, L. S., Clark, L. J., & Moriarty, C. L. (2019). The efficacy of hypnosis as a treatment for anxiety: A meta-analysis. *International Journal of Clinical and Experimental Hypnosis*, *67*(3), 336–363. https://doi.org/10.1080/00207144.2019.1613863

Weir, K. (2024). Uncovering the new science of clinical hypnosis. *Monitor on Psychology*, *55*(3), https://www.apa.org/monitor/2024/04/science-of-hypnosis

Chapter 7
How Do I Know if I Can Be Hypnotized?

Gary Elkins
Cameron Alldredge

We know from numerous research studies that *everyone* has the ability to benefit from hypnotherapy. However, it is also true that some people need more sessions to achieve the same benefit or may need hypnotic suggestions that are more individualized to achieve their goals. This difference in hypnotic abilities is referred to as *hypnotizability*.

There are several older terms referencing hypnotic ability that you may have heard of such as *susceptibility* or *suggestibility*. The terms were used in the past (and are still sometimes used) because some early researchers in the 1800s and mid-1960s thought that people who have an ability to experience hypnosis were in some way more "susceptible" to hypnosis or just more "suggestible" than others. However, we now know that these older ideas are inaccurate. First, it is important to keep in mind that experiencing hypnosis is something *you learn to do*, not something that is done to you. People are not susceptible to hypnosis the way they may be susceptible to catching a cold or virus. Second, research has shown that hypnotizability and suggestibility are very different concepts. People who are higher in hypnotic ability (or hypnotizability) are not more "suggestible" in the sense that they are more prone to be influenced by marketing and advertisements or being persuaded by peers.

Hypnotizability is defined as an individual's ***ability*** to experience suggested alterations in physiology, sensations, emotions, thoughts, or behaviors during hypnosis. This is the official definition of the American Psychological Association's Division of Psychological Hypnosis. It emphasizes that hypnotizability is an ability or trait. People who have greater hypnotizability are more easily able to use self-hypnosis or hypnotherapy to manage pain, reduce stress, or alter habits when they choose to do so.

What Are the Facts About Hypnotizability?

Research has shown that hypnotizability is normally distributed in the adult population. This means that about 10% of people are in the lower range; about 10% are in the very high range; and most of us (about 80%) are average or in the mid-range. Everyone has hypnotic ability, while the level of ability varies so some are higher and some are lower. You can think about hypnotizability like intelligence quotient (IQ). Everyone has intelligence, but not to the same degree. Some people score very high in intelligence while others score low; however, most people score somewhere in the middle.

Hypnotizability can be reliably measured with several well validated scales. These include the Elkins Hypnotizability Scale, the Hypnotic Induction Profile, the Harvard Group Scale, and the Stanford Scales, just to name a few. These scales of hypnotizability are most often used in scientific research, however, they are also commonly used in therapy settings. Knowing a person's level of hypnotizability can inform clinicians on what the best approach will be for treatment and help them estimate the number of sessions necessary to reach treatment goals.

What Traits Are Associated with Hypnotizability?

There are several characteristics that are associated with hypnotizability:

- People who are more *intelligent* tend to be more hypnotizable.

- People who can become *absorbed* in reading a book or watching a movie tend to have more hypnotic abilities.

- People who are more *creative* tend to be more hypnotizable.

- People with a good ability to use their *imagination* score higher on standardized scales of hypnotizability.

- People who are higher in *empathy* for self and others tend to have more hypnotic abilities.

- People with *positive expectations* for experiencing hypnosis tend to score higher on scales of hypnotizability.

- People who are *motivated* to experience hypnosis score somewhat higher on hypnotizability scales.

- People who *believe* they can experience hypnosis (based on past experience with mental imagery, meditation, or hypnosis) are more likely to be correct in their estimation compared to people who have never experienced mental imagery, mediation, or hypnosis.

- People who are more *mentally healthy* tend to be more hypnotizable.

What if I'm in the Lower Range of Hypnotizability?

If you are in the lower range of hypnotizability, do not be concerned! You can still use hypnosis and greatly benefit from hypnotherapy. You should not feel discouraged at all. In hypnotherapy, this simply means that you may need more sessions and more frequent practice of self-hypnosis to achieve your goals. You should remain confident and remember that even with hypnosis, *persistence pays off*. In the same way a person with less musical talent can still learn to play an instrument, a person who falls into the lower range of hypnotizability can learn to use hypnosis to their benefit—it just may require more practice!

Can I Test My Hypnotizability at Home?

There is a short test that you can take to self-assess your hypnotizability. This test is called the BREATH test (the full name is the *Brief Remote Elkins-Alldredge Test of Hypnotizability*). It takes about 5–10 minutes can be found online at: mindsethealth.com/topic/self-tests-quizzes.

Additionally, you can get an idea of your likely hypnotizability score by completing the following questionnaire. The questions are based on the things that are correlated or related to hypnotizability. They do not give an exact score, but you can get a general idea for what your score may be on the BREATH or other scales of hypnotizability.

ESTIMATING YOUR HYPNOTIZABILITY QUESTIONNAIRE

1. How intelligent are you?
   Low | Average | High

2. How creative are you?
   Low | Average | High

3. How much empathy do you have for yourself and others?
   Low | Average | High

4. How good is your ability to imagine things and use mental imagery?
   Low | Average | High

5. How well can you become absorbed in a book or watching a movie?
   Low | Average | High

6. How well can you "let go" and allow things to happen vs. being controlling?
   Low | Average | High

7. Have you ever experienced a state of consciousness like hypnosis?
   No | Maybe | Yes

8. How motivated are you to experience a hypnotic state?
   None | A Little | Very Much

9. What level of hypnotizability do you guess you might have?
   Low | Average | High

Scoring: If you answered *Low*, *No*, or *None* on most items, you are likely in the lower range. If you answered *Average* or *A Little* to most items and *Yes* or *High* to some items, you are likely in the average range. If you answered *High*, *Very Much*, or *Yes* to most items, you are probably more highly hypnotizable.

Summary

Hypnotizability is a talent or ability that does not change a great deal over time. Everyone is hypnotizable to some degree which is why anyone can benefit from hypnotherapy. Some of the things that correlate with higher hypnotizability include intelligence, ability for absorption, creativity, imagery ability, empathy, positive expectancy, and motivation. It is helpful to know one's level of hypnotizability to create a more individualized approach for treatment. You can take a brief self-assessment test of hypnotizability online at mindsethealth.com/topic/self-tests-quizzes.

REFERENCES

Alexander, J. E., Stimpson, K. H., Kittle, J., & Spiegel, D. (2021). The Hypnotic Induction Profile (HIP) in clinical practice and research. *International Journal of Clinical and Experimental Hypnosis, 69*(1), 72-82. https://doi.org/10.1080/00207144.2021.1836646

Alldredge, C. T., Sliwinski, J. R., & Elkins, G. R. (2024). Treating hot flashes with hypnosis: Does hypnotizability modulate reductions? *Journal of Clinical Psychology in Medical Settings, 31*(2), 465–470. https://doi.org/10.1007/s10880-023-09994-w

Barnier, A.J., & McConkey, K.M. (2004). Defining and identifying the highly hypnotizable person. In M. Heap, R. Brown, & D. Oakley (Eds.), *The highly hypnotizable person: Theoretical, experimental and clinical issues* (pp. 30-60). New York, NY: Brunner Routledge.

Bates, B. (1993) Individual differences in response to hypnosis. In J. W. Rhue, S. J. Luynn, & I. Kirsch (Eds), *Handbook of clinical hypnosis* (pp. 23-54). American Psychological Association.

Elkins, G. (2022) *Introduction to clinical hypnosis: The basics and beyond.* Mountain Pine Publishing.

Elkins, G. R., Barabasz, A. F., Council, J. R., & Spiegel, D. (2015). Advancing research and practice: The revised APA Division 30 definition of hypnosis. *The International Journal of Clinical and Experimental Hypnosis, 63*(1), 1–9. https://doi.org/10.1080/00207144.2014.961870

Elkins, G., Fisher, W., & Johnson, A. (2012). P02.30. Assessment of hypnotizability in clinical research: Development, reliability, and validation of the Elkins Hypnotizability Scale. *BMC Complementary and Alternative Medicine, 12*(Suppl 1), P86. https://doi.org/10.1186/1472-6882-12-S1-P86

Elkins, G., Fisher, W., Johnson, A., Marcus, J., Dove, J., Perfect, M., & Keith, T. (2011). Moderate effect of hypnotizability on hypnosis for hot flashes in breast cancer survivors. *Contemporary Hypnosis & Integrative Therapy, 28*(3), 187–195.

Flammer, E., & Bongartz, W. (2003). On the efficacy of hypnosis: A meta-analytic study. *Contemporary Hypnosis, 20*(4), 179–197. https://doi.org/10.1002/ch.277

Hilgard, E. R. (1965). *Hypnotic susceptibility*. Harcourt, Brace & World. https://doi.org/10.1146/annurev.ps.36.020185.002125

Kekecs, Z., Bowers, J., Johnson, A., Kendrick, C., & Elkins, G. (2016). The Elkins Hypnotizability Scale: Assessment of reliability and validity. *International Journal of Clinical and Experimental Hypnosis, 64*(3), 285-304. https://doi.org/10.1080/00207144.2016.1171089

Kekecs, Z., Roberts, L., Na, H., Yek, M. H., Slonena, E. E., Racelis, E., Voor, T. A., Johansson, R., Rizzo, P., Csikos, E., Vizkievicz, V., & Elkins, G. (2021). Test-retest reliability of the Stanford Hypnotic Susceptibility Scale, Form C and the Elkins Hypnotizability Scale. *The International Journal of Clinical and Experimental Hypnosis, 69*(1), 142–161. https://doi.org/10.1080/00207144.2021.1834858

Kihlstrom, J. F. (1985). Hypnosis. *Annual Review of Psychology, 36*, 385-418. https://doi.org/10.1146/annurev.ps.36.020185.002125

Elkins, G., Fisher, W., Johnson, A., Marcus, J., Dove, J., Perfect, M., & Keith, T. (2011). Moderating effect of hypnotizability on hypnosis for hot flashes in breast cancer survivors. *Contemporary Hypnosis & Integrative Therapy, 28*(3), 187–195.

Montgomery, G. H., David, D., Winkel, G., Silverstein, J. H., & Bovbjerg, D. H. (2002). The effectiveness of adjunctive hypnosis with surgical patients: a meta-analysis. *Anesthesia and Analgesia, 94*(6). https://doi.org/10.1097/00000539-200206000-00052

Morgan, A.H. (1973). The heritability of hypnotic susceptibility in twins. *Journal of Abnormal Psychology, 82*(1), 55-61. https://doi.org/10.1037/h0034854

Patterson, D. R., & Jensen, M. P. (2003). Hypnosis and clinical pain. *Psychological Bulletin, 129*(4), 495-521. https://doi.org/10.1037/0033-2909.129.4.495

Piccione, C., Hilgard, E.R., Zimbardo, P.G. (1989). On the degree of stability of measured hypnotizability over a 25-year period. *Journal of Personality and Social Psychology, 56*(2), 289-295. https://doi.org/10.1037//0022-3514.56.2.289

Tasso, A. F., & Pérez, N. A. (2008). Parsing everyday suggestibility: What does it tell us about hypnosis? In M. R. Nash & A. J. Barnier (Eds.), *The Oxford handbook of hypnosis: Theory, research, and practice* (pp. 283–309). Oxford University Press.

Tasso, A.F., Pérez, N.A., Moore, M., Griffo, R., & Nash, M.R. (2020). Hypnotic responsiveness and nonhypnotic suggestibility: Disparate, similar, or the same? *International Journal of Clinical and Experimental Hypnosis, 68*(1), 38-67. https://doi.org/10.1080/00207144.2020.1685330

Woody, E., & Sadler, P. (2016). Hypnotizability. In G.R. Elkins (Ed.), *Handbook of medical and psychological hypnosis: Foundations, applications, and professional issues* (pp. 35-41). New York, NY: Springer Publishing Company.

Yek, M. H., & Elkins, G. R. (2021). Therapeutic use of the Elkins Hypnotizability Scale: A feasibility study. *International Journal of Clinical and Experimental Hypnosis, 69*(1), 124–141. https://doi.org/10.1080/00207144.2021.1831390

Chapter 8
Smoking Cessation

Gary Elkins
Vindhya Ekanayake

Virtually everyone knows that smoking is bad for your health. However, many people do not mindfully think about the devastating effects of cigarette smoking on health, disease, and death. Cigarette smoking is the leading cause of preventable death and disease in the United States. It is estimated that cigarette smoking causes 1 in 5 deaths every year. This means that 480,000 deaths every year are due, directly or indirectly, to tobacco use. Most smoking-related deaths are caused by lung cancer and chronic obstructive pulmonary disease (COPD; also known as emphysema). In chronic smokers, the likelihood of experiencing cardiovascular disease or stroke is doubled to quadrupled when compared to people who do not smoke. Smoking can negatively impact sexual performance and health: there is a relationship between smoking and erectile dysfunction (e.g., impotence) in men and infertility in women (including secondhand smoke exposure). Smoking is also associated with sleep difficulties, insomnia, diabetes, gum disease, high blood pressure, and pain signals in the body.

In 2021, nearly 12 of every 100 U.S. adults aged 18 years or older (11.5%) smoked cigarettes, meaning an estimated 28.3 million adults in the United States currently smoke cigarettes. More than 16 million Americans live with a smoking-related disease.

In 2020, about 8.5% of individuals in the U.S. aged 12 or older had a diagnosis of tobacco use disorder (based on the past month). From 1960 to 2020, approximately 29.5 million Americans have died from smoking. On average, a smoker will live a decade less than an individual who does not smoke.

There is a pressing need to help more people stop smoking. It is challenging to quit smoking and highly improbable without some kind of help. Evidence supports hypnotherapy, as well as some medications like nicotine replacement, to aid in the cessation of smoking. We will review the evidence for hypnotherapy, how it works for smoking cessation, and the Finito app for stopping smoking with hypnotherapy. Since some people use nicotine replacement therapy and/or medications in conjunction with hypnotherapy, we will discuss those as well.

Hypnotherapy for Smoking Cessation

Hypnosis for smoking cessation has many benefits. Hypnotherapy involves learning about ways to stop smoking, daily self-hypnosis sessions, and support from family and friends. Hypnotherapy increases an individual's motivation to stop smoking, heightens confidence in one's ability to quit, and aids in managing cravings. In some ways, hypnotherapy has some aspects of both *motivational interviewing* and *cognitive-behavioral therapy*. In the initial phases of hypnotherapy, the individual is guided to consider the advantages and disadvantages of smoking for themselves. This can help increase motivation as one becomes more aware of the health risks and disadvantages of smoking. Also, in hypnotherapy, like in cognitive-behavioral therapy, smokers learn to cope with emotions and beliefs that lead them to smoke and learn relapse prevention strategies. Hypnotherapy puts everything together in a way that works and is easy for an individual to use in the "real world." Hypnotherapy for smoking cessation, including via the Finito app, usually involves three stages:

- **Week 1: Getting Ready to Quit Smoking**
  - Learning information about how to stop smoking.
  - Using self-hypnosis for stress management.
  - Building your support system.
  - Increasing your motivation.
  - Setting a date to stop smoking.
  - Developing a strong sense of confidence and belief in yourself.
  - Getting rid of cigarettes.
  - Daily self-hypnosis sessions.

- **Week 2: Stopping Smoking and Withdrawal**
  - Stop smoking date.
  - Self-hypnosis to reduce and cope with withdrawal symptoms.
  - Reducing cravings with hypnotherapy.
  - Improving your sleep.
  - Coping with stress.
  - Mobilizing your support system.
  - Learning to relax and stay calm.

- **Week 3: Becoming a Non-Smoker-Free from Cigarettes**
  - Daily self-hypnosis sessions.
  - Special hypnosis sessions to relax and sleep well.
  - Confidence and belief in yourself as you grow stronger.
  - Visualization of life as a non-smoker.
  - Developing new habits.
  - Identifying your triggers.
  - Moving into the maintenance stage and remaining a non-smoker, free from cigarettes.

What the Science Says about Hypnosis for Smoking Cessation

A recent meta-analysis comprised of 261 different studies on hypnosis for the treatment of various psychological and physical health conditions found that hypnosis for smoking cessation can be extremely effective. A systematic review comprised of 63 studies found the effects of hypnotherapy on smoking cessation to be very positive. A subset of the studies (approximately 67%) reported a very positive impact of the hypnosis intervention for smoking cessation.

The research indicates that a single session of hypnosis is not very effective, with less than 20% of individuals quitting cigarettes after one session. However, with a well-organized hypnotherapy program, the success rate goes up exponentially. The optimal hypnotherapy program for smoking cessation is more intensive and includes staying with the hypnotherapy program for least 3 weeks, daily self-hypnosis sessions, psychoeducation about stopping smoking, setting a quit date, good social support, and reducing stress. With this type of hypnotherapy, most people can stop smoking. It is important to remember: *persistence pays off!*

Research has found that intensive hypnotherapy delivered by use of an app can achieve results as high as those from individual, in-person sessions. The Finito app is a program developed by Dr. Gary Elkins, in conjunction with Mindset Health. The Finito app is a very beneficial, pleasant, and cost-effective method for stopping smoking. A retrospective study that examined preliminary survey data from users of the Finito app found 76% of users either significantly reduced or stopped smoking completely. More than 50% had stopped smoking after 3 weeks of using the Finito app. It is equally impressive that frequently reported secondary benefits of smoking cessation among survey respondents were reduced spending, improved sleep quality, and greater levels of relaxation.

Individuals interested in hypnotherapy may consider the Finito app, as it has the advantages of low cost compared to in-person sessions, can be used at home, and allows for tracking progress using daily recordings of number of cigarettes smoked.

Digital Hypnotherapy to Reduce or Stop Smoking

The Finito app is a 21-day digital hypnotherapy program that provides psychoeducation about a variety of issues related to smoking cessation as well as daily self-hypnosis sessions that are 15-minutes in length. The Finito program is based on research that investigated intensive hypnotherapy for smoking cessation. More information about the app can be found at tryfinito.com.

The initial part of the program involves an orientation, psycho-education on cravings and triggers, how to reduce cigarette use, and getting ready to quit. During the second phase, users of the app are guided on how to progressively cut down on the number of cigarettes smoked and set a date to stop smoking completely. Finito users also learn strategies for managing cravings, reducing stress, and dealing with social situations. In the final week of the program, users of the app learn relapse prevention strategies as well as ways to build new habits into their lives. Finito users are also provided with a toolkit to cope with cravings and educational readings on a diverse array of topics, including how smoking and anxiety are related, and how to manage setbacks in their journey to stopping smoking. The app includes a cigarette tracker, as well as a reinforcement program for users following completion of the main portions of the overall program. The Finito app for smoking cessation can be used alone or in conjunction with nicotine replacement therapy or other pharmacotherapies, such as Chantix (varenicline) or Wellbutrin (bupropion).

Case Example – Charles

Charles was a 53-year-old married man who started smoking when he was 16 years old. He stated, "Everyone I know smoked back then." He initially only smoked occasionally when going out with friends and for relaxation. He stated that he just began smoking more over the years, until at age 24 he was smoking a pack a day. However, he was physically active, working as a carpenter, and usually went to the gym twice a week and did weightlifting. He was married at age 26 and at that time his 23-year-old wife did not smoke.

As the years passed, Charles began to smoke more, until at age 50 he was smoking two or more packs of cigarettes per day. He stated that his wife had also picked up smoking and she was probably smoking about a pack of cigarettes per day. He stated that they had an adult son and a daughter, and that neither of them smoked. Charles stated that he now has 3 grandchildren (ages 3–6 years old) who "want Papa to stop smoking."

Charles stated that he had tried to stop smoking on his own several times in the past. He was able to stop smoking for a few days using nicotine patches, but then resumed smoking as he had before. However, he noticed that he was experiencing more shortness of breath, including when walking up flights of stairs, and at work. Charles stated that the turning point came last year when he saw his physician, who told him he was developing COPD and was at risk for lung or throat cancer. He stated, "I knew I needed to stop smoking." His doctor recommended that he try hypnotherapy using the Finito app program.

Charles did not know anything about hypnosis. However, he read about the Finito app and signed up for a free trial. He found the hypnosis sessions to be very relaxing, and the information on how to get ready to stop smoking made sense to him. Also, his wife listened to a few sessions and decided she would join him in this "stop smoking journey." They listened to some of the hypnotherapy sessions together, and some on their own. After the first 6 days, they had both stopped smoking. The hypnotherapy sessions helped reduce stress, and they usually had a session in the morning and a session at night. They both found the "reduce craving toolkit" helpful in coping with withdrawal symptoms. Their children and grandchildren were supportive. Charles thought about using a nicotine patch, but felt he did not need it, and his confidence increased as he and his wife became non-smokers. They renewed their Finito program so they could continue the hypnosis sessions as needed.

They both found their sleep was improved and stress reduced with the hypnosis sessions.

Medications and Smoking Cessation

As noted above, hypnotherapy can be combined with medications such as nicotine patches or gum. If the combined approach helps you, that's great! While Charles did not feel he needed any additional medications, nicotine replacement therapy (NRT) can be a helpful adjunctive medication for stopping smoking. The FDA has approved five NRT products: patch, gum, lozenge, oral inhaler, and nasal spray, and they can usually be obtained without a prescription. Smoking cessation rates for NRTs range from 15.7% to 23.9%, and a typical length of treatment is 12 weeks.

In 2006, varenicline, another type of medication, was approved by the FDA for smoking cessation. This medication functions similarly to nicotine, in that it leads to the release of the neurotransmitter dopamine. However, it may have risks for some individuals. In the 2000s, the FDA placed a product label warning on varenicline for potential neuropsychiatric and cardiovascular effects. The warning label was removed in 2016 following a clinical trial that did not find evidence for these side effects.

Bupropion is an antidepressant medication that is sometimes prescribed for smoking cessation. Bupropion (also known by its brand name of Wellbutrin) is believed to work by blocking the reuptake of the neurotransmitters dopamine and noradrenaline in the brain. This medication may decrease the withdrawal symptoms that can occur once an individual stops smoking. Bupropion is typically taken one week before an individual's quit date and beyond. It can have side effects such as dry mouth, irritability, and restlessness, but can still be a useful adjunctive medication for some people. Certainly, it can be used in combination with hypnotherapy if desired or recommended by a health care provider.

Summary

In this chapter, we have discussed that hypnotherapy can be very effective in helping people stop smoking. The most effective hypnotherapy programs involve multiple sessions of at least 3 weeks, daily self-hypnosis sessions, psychoeducation about stopping smoking, setting a quit date, encouraging good social support, and including self-hypnosis sessions for stress reduction. The research evidence for hypnotherapy is very encouraging and most people who complete a full hypnotherapy program significantly reduce or stop smoking altogether. The most important things to remember are to be persistent, don't give up, and to have daily hypnotherapy sessions. The Finito app from Mindset Health provides a 21-day research-based program that can be used as a standalone treatment or in combination with medications to quit smoking. With the Finito app, 70% of individuals who completed the program significantly reduced or stopped smoking completely. You can find more information about hypnotherapy for smoking cessation and the Finito app at: tryfinito.com.

REFERENCES

Alldredge, C. T., Muñiz, V., Ekanayake, V., & Elkins, G. R. (2024). Preliminary survey data from an app-delivered hypnosis intervention for smoking cessation. *Tobacco Use Insights*, *17*. https://doi.org/10.1177/1179173X241287398

Carney, G., Bassett, K., Maclure, M., Taylor, S., & Dormuth, C. R. (2020). Cardiovascular and neuropsychiatric safety of smoking cessation pharmacotherapies in non-depressed adults: A retrospective cohort study. *Addiction*, *115*(8), 1534–1546. https://doi.org/10.1111/add.14951

Centers for Disease Control and Prevention. (2023, May 4). *Current cigarette smoking among adults in the United States*. U.S. Department of Health and Human Services. https://www.cdc.gov/tobacco/php/data-statistics/adult-data-cigarettes

Ekanayake, V. & Elkins, G.R. (in press). Systematic review on hypnotherapy and smoking cessation. *International Journal of Clinical and Experimental Hypnosis*.

Elkins, G.R., & Rajab, H. (2004) Clinical hypnosis for smoking cessation: Preliminary results of a three-session intervention. *International Journal of Clinical and Experimental Hypnosis, 52*, 73-81. https://doi.org/10.1076/iceh.52.1.73.23921

Elkins, G.R., Marcus, J.D., Bates, J., & Palamara, L. (2006) Intensive hypnotherapy for smoking cessation: A prospective study. *International Journal of Clinical and Experimental Hypnosis, 54*(3), 303-315. https://doi.org/10.1080/00207140600689512

Elkins, G.R. and Perfect, M. (2007). Hypnosis for health compromising behaviors, In Nash, M., (Ed.), *The Oxford Handbook of Hypnosis*. Oxford, United Kingdom: Oxford Medical Publications.

Green, J. P., & Lynn, S. J. (2017). Smoking cessation. In G. R. Elkins (Ed.), *Handbook of medical and psychological hypnosis: Foundations, applications, and professional issues* (pp. 621–628). Springer Publishing Co.

Guo, K., Zhou, L., Shang, X., Yang, C., E, F., Wang, Y., Xu, M., Wu, Y., Li, Y., Li, M., Yang,

K., & Li, X. (2022). Varenicline and related interventions on smoking cessation: A systematic review and network meta-analysis. *Drug and Alcohol Dependence, 241*, 109672. https://doi.org/10.1016/j.drugalcdep.2022.109672

Hawk, L. W., Ashare, R. L., Rhodes, J. D., Oliver, J. A., Cummings, K. M., & Mahoney, M. C. (2015). Does extended pre quit bupropion aid in extinguishing smoking behavior? *Nicotine & Tobacco Research, 17*(11), 1377–1384. https://doi.org/10.1093/ntr/ntu347

Jha, P. (2020). The hazards of smoking and the benefits of cessation: A critical summation of the epidemiological evidence in high-income countries. *eLife, 9*, e49979. https://doi.org/10.7554/eLife.49979

National Institute on Drug Abuse. (2020, January). *Research report: What is the scope of tobacco, nicotine, and e-cigarette use in the United States?* National Institutes of Health.

Patnode, C. D., Henderson, J. T., Coppola, E. L., Melnikow, J., Durbin, S., & Thomas, R. G. (2021). Interventions for tobacco cessation in adults, including pregnant persons: Updated evidence report and systematic review for the US Preventive Services Task Force. *JAMA, 325*(3), 280. https://doi.org/10.1001/jama.2020.23541

Rigotti, N. A., Kruse, G. R., Livingstone-Banks, J., & Hartmann-Boyce, J. (2022). Treatment of tobacco smoking: A review. *JAMA, 327*(6), 566. https://doi.org/10.1001/jama.2022.0395

Rosendahl, J., Alldredge, C. T., & Haddenhorst, A. (2024). Meta-analytic evidence on the efficacy of hypnosis for mental and somatic health issues: A 20-year perspective. *Frontiers in Psychology, 14*, 1330238. https://doi.org/10.3389/fpsyg.2023.1330238

Chapter 9
Menopause and Women's Health: Hot Flashes and Sleep

GARY ELKINS

VANESSA MUÑIZ

At age 50, Courtney had her first hot flash. At first, she simply tried to ignore the symptoms of menopause. However, by age 52, she was having up to 15 hot flashes a day, which caused anxiety, sleep problems, and was very disruptive to her day-to-day functioning. Doctors refer to these hot flashes as "vasomotor symptoms," because they result in sweating, chills, and facial flushing. Additionally, Courtney experienced hot flashes that occurred at night, known as "night sweats," which interfered with her sleep.

Courtney's sleep and anxiety progressively worsened throughout the following months, causing a significant disruption in her day-to-day activities. She tried using fans during the days and ice packs under her pillow at night. However, none of these things worked to control the hot flashes. It was then that she had a conversation with her primary care physician. Courtney's doctor reviewed her family history and helped her decide how to best manage her menopausal symptoms. Courtney's mother was diagnosed with breast cancer in her early 60s and that was a concern for Courtney as well. Her doctor explained that hormone therapy (estrogen + progesterone replacement) increased the risk of cardiovascular disease, stroke, and breast cancer. Therefore, alternative options, such as antidepressant medications, were discussed. The other option her doctor discussed with her was hypnotherapy to reduce hot flashes, improve sleep, and manage stress. Courtney decided to try hypnotherapy.

After five weeks of daily self-hypnosis sessions with the Evia app, Courtney's hot flashes had decreased by over 70%. The hot flashes became less frequent and less severe. She usually did a self-hypnosis session before going to bed. As a result, her night sweats nearly vanished, her sleep quality and mood improved, and the nagging sense of stress and anxiety was mostly gone.

Courtney's experience with hypnotherapy for menopausal symptoms was far from unusual. In fact, research indicates that most women can reduce their hot flashes by a clinically significant amount and improve their sleep with daily self-hypnosis sessions. In this chapter you will learn:

1. What causes hot flashes?
2. What are the risks and benefits of hormone replacement therapy (HRT) (estrogen + progesterone)?
3. Why do breast cancer survivors have hot flashes?
4. What are some alternatives to HRT?
5. What does the science tell us about the efficacy of hypnotherapy for hot flashes and sleep?
6. How does the Evia app work to reduce hot flashes and improve sleep in menopause?

What Causes Hot Flashes?

Hot flashes occur when estrogen levels decline. This can be due to natural menopause (onset is usually around age 52), if ovaries are surgically removed, or following treatment for breast cancer. Hot flashes are transient and spontaneous sensations of intense heat, sweating, and flushing felt primarily in the chest, face, and neck, and night sweats are hot flashes experienced during the night. They are both commonly accompanied by heart palpitations, headaches, fatigue, anxiety, chills, and have been extensively reported across large surveys to negatively impact the health and quality of life of the women experiencing them. Because of night sweats, most women transitioning into menopause might also experience poor sleep quality on top of the stress caused by menopause-related symptoms.

Hot flashes are a dysregulation of core body temperature. Core body temperature is regulated by the *hypothalamus,* which is a part of the brain that is affected by changes in hormone levels and triggers sweating when there is a perception of excessive heat. When the hypothalamus triggers a hot flash, it attempts to cool the person by sweating. For this reason, hot flashes are often followed by "cold sweats." After the onset of menopause, the hypothalamus eventually begins to regulate core body temperature normally again, but this can take about 5–10 years without hypnotherapy. Hypnotherapy can help regulate core body temperature by introducing mental images for coolness (i.e. imagery such as snow or a cool breeze), suggesting calmness, and improving sleep. Rather than taking years for hot flashes to reduce on their own, daily practice of self-hypnosis can bring about regulation of body temperature within a month.

What are the Risks and Benefits of Hormone Replacement Therapy (HRT) (Estrogen + Progesterone)?

The most common treatment for hot flashes is hormone therapy. During hormone therapy, women receive either estrogen and progestin, or estrogen alone, for the reduction of hot flashes. HRT reduces hot flash frequency by up to 75% and improves hot flash severity by up to 87%. However, 50% of women experience a relapse in vasomotor symptoms after stopping hormone therapy. The benefits of HRT include reduction of hot flashes, improved bone health, better sleep, and reduced risk of colorectal cancer. However, these benefits must be balanced by consideration of the risks for postmenopausal women, including increased chance of developing breast cancer and cardiovascular disease (i.e., heart attack or stroke). For example, in the largest study examining risk factors associated with hormone therapy published to date involving over 16,000 women post-menopause, those taking hormone therapy had a significantly greater occurrence of coronary heart disease, breast cancer, strokes, and blood clots in the legs and lungs. In some cases, the risk was greater in women over 60 years of age, or those more than 10 years past menopause. Therefore, many physicians recommend women reduce their use of estrogen (hormone therapy), taper to the lowest effective dose, and consider non-hormonal therapies. It is a decision that is best made on an individual basis, as some women are at higher risk (those with a family history of breast cancer or heart disease) while other women may be at a relatively low risk. The Evia app for hot flashes can be used alone or in conjunction with hormone therapy or other non-hormonal therapies, such as anti-anxiety or antidepressant medications.

Why Do Breast Cancer Survivors Have Hot Flashes?

Up to 81% of breast cancer survivors suffer from early induced hot flashes. Approximately 200,000 women are diagnosed with breast cancer each year, and most will have severe hot flashes. The treatment for breast cancer often includes surgery, radiation, and chemotherapy. These treatments can be stressful, and most women become concerned about the recurrence of breast cancer in the years following successful treatment. Breast cancer, in a sense, "feeds" on estrogen (however it is not caused by estrogen). Therefore, most breast cancer survivors are prescribed medications that prevent estrogen production. These medications are known to often lead to hot flashes and early menopause. Even if the woman is young, the onset of menopause can occur in a matter of days and hot flashes can be very frequent and particularly severe for breast cancer survivors.

CHAPTER 9: MENOPAUSE AND WOMEN'S HEALTH:
HOT FLASHES AND SLEEP

The medications that are prescribed to "shut down" estrogen production include a class of drugs known as selective estrogen-receptor modulators (SERMs) or aromatase inhibitors. The medications most often prescribed include tamoxifen or raloxifene (SERMs). The most commonly prescribed aromatase inhibitors include exemestane, letrozole, and anastrozole. Approximately 90% of postmenopausal women with a history of breast cancer who receive both chemotherapy and medications to "shut down" all estrogen production experience hot flashes and night sweats. Since breast cancer survivors cannot take estrogen (HRT), there is a need for non-hormonal alternatives.

What Are Some Alternatives to HRT?

Alternatives to hormone replacement therapy include non-hormonal drugs, such as paroxetine (e.g., Brisdelle) and venlafaxine (e.g., Effexor), the anticonvulsant medication gabapentin (e.g., Neurontin, Gralise, Horizant), or clonidine (e.g., Catapres). Percentage of hot flash reduction varies depending on the type of population and medication (many are antidepressants) observed. For example, in studies reporting a significant reduction of hot flashes, paroxetine, venlafaxine, and fluoxetine have had a 41%, 33%, and 13% reduction of hot flashes in menopausal women, respectively. Unlike hormone therapy, they are not associated with risk of breast cancer, or breast cancer reoccurrence. However, most of them can have undesirable side effects.

Gabapentin has been reported across clinical trials to have about a 30% to 38% reduction of hot flashes, and studies on Clonidine have reported an even smaller reduction or benefit for the treatment of hot flashes. Moreover, significant side effects such as nausea, difficulty sleeping or drowsiness, weight gain, weakness, and blurred vision might discourage some women from using these treatments before they have first tried non-pharmacological treatment options.

In 2023, fezolinetant (Veozah) was approved by the FDA for the treatment of severe hot flashes. Fezolinetant blocks the brain activity regulating body temperature and therefore decreases the onset of hot flashes. This medication could potentially be an alternative to hormone replacement therapy and studies have reported a clinically significant decrease in hot flash frequency. However, the drug's long-term efficacy and its effects on women with hypertension, cardiovascular problems, or breast cancer survivors also need to be studied. Currently, possible side effects include headaches in low doses and abdominal pain, nausea, vomiting, colitis, and hematochezia in higher doses. Additionally, fezolinetant is generally not recommended for women with a history of cirrhosis, impaired renal function, or end-stage renal disease.

Psychological treatments for hot flashes such as cognitive-behavioral therapy (CBT) and mindfulness meditation have also been studied. Approximately 50% of women experiencing menopausal symptoms try some form of psychological treatment for the reduction of vasomotor symptoms. According to the North American Menopause Society, the most common behavioral treatments for hot flashes include hypnotherapy, CBT, or mindfulness-based interventions (MBI). From these interventions, only hypnotherapy has enough evidence for its recommendation as a treatment to reduce hot flashes and improve sleep by 70% or more.

Clinical research on the benefits of mindfulness-based interventions (including meditation, body awareness, and yoga) shows that these therapies can help a person to relax but do not significantly reduce hot flashes. Cognitive Behavioral Therapy (CBT) is well-known, but does not reduce the frequency and severity of hot flashes by a clinically significant amount. Similar to mindfulness, meditation, or yoga, CBT can help women to cope with hot flashes and daily interference but it does not decrease them by any clinically significant amount. Only hypnotherapy has been proven to be an effective behavioral treatment by reducing hot flash frequency and severity. Therefore, CBT can be a possible treatment option for women interested in solely treating psychological concerns caused by hot flashes. Hypnotherapy, on the other hand, is an

Chapter 9: Menopause and Women's Health: Hot Flashes and Sleep

intervention that has been shown to significantly reduce hot flashes by 70% to 80%, improve sleep, and reduce stress.

Hypnotherapy for Hot Flashes: What the Science Says

Hypnotherapy is the only behavioral treatment that has been shown to be effective for the clinically significant reduction of hot flash frequency and severity while also providing psychological benefits. Randomized clinical trials of hypnotherapy have shown that it reduces the frequency, severity, and bother of hot flashes by approximately 70–80% and improves sleep quality by over 50%. Moreover, hypnotherapy is the only behavioral treatment in which physiologically measured hot flashes (not just self-report questionnaires and daily diaries) are significantly reduced.

The graph here shows the average reduction of hot flashes that participants reported while using hypnotherapy. These findings are based on results from our most recent randomized controlled trial which included over 180 participants. As you can see, improvements were noticeable after just two weeks and continued to decrease through the treatment program and the 12-week follow-up.

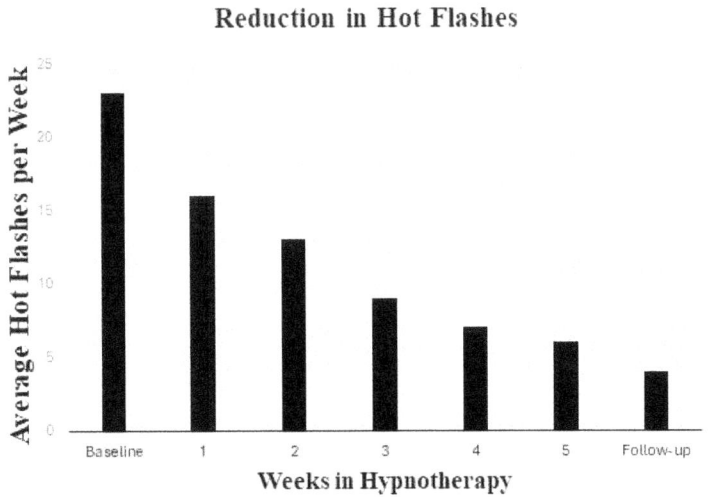

The efficacy of hypnotherapy for reduction in hot flashes has been compared to Gabapentin and antidepressants. In in one study participants received either hypnotherapy or Gabapentin medication. Those that received hypnotherapy reduced their daily number of hot flashes by 80%,. On the other hand, the participants receiving Gabapentin experienced a 33.3% reduction in the frequency and severity of hot flashes.

Hypnotherapy for hot flashes can be delivered through the Evia app. Research has also found that the Evia app, which delivers daily self-hypnosis sessions, had outcomes comparable to in-person hypnotherapy, with 70% of users achieving a clinically significant reduction in hot flashes. Women interested in hypnotherapy may consider the Evia app, as it has the advantages of lower cost compared to in-person sessions, can be used at home, and allows for tracking progress using daily recordings of hot flashes and sleep.

Digital Hypnotherapy for Hot Flashes and Sleep

The Evia app is a 5-week digital hypnotherapy program that provides psychoeducation about menopause and daily self-hypnosis sessions (usually 15 to 20 minutes in length). The Evia program is based upon the published work of Dr. Gary Elkins and randomized clinical trials of hypnotherapy for hot flashes. The self-hypnosis sessions include mental imagery for coolness, such as suggestions to visualize a snowy mountain path, a cold lake, a frosty morning, or suggestions to encourage the user to picture themselves walking in summer rain, eating a cool treat, or entering an air-conditioned room. In addition, users also receive guidance and suggestions to practice self-hypnosis and are encouraged to track their hot flashes and potential triggers. These additional items empower patients to regain control and equip them with the tools necessary to manage their hot flash symptoms.

The Evia app also includes guidance and self-hypnosis sessions to improve sleep. This generally involves tracking progress in improving sleep quality, listening to a self-hypnosis session before going to sleep, and good sleep hygiene. The hypnosis sessions for sleep include hypnotic suggestions and mental imagery for deeper sleep, and ways to go back to sleep following any night-time awakenings.

As stated earlier, everyone can benefit from hypnotherapy. Research on hypnotherapy for hot flashes has shown that even individuals with lower-than-average hypnotizability achieved a significant reduction in hot flashes. The most important thing is to complete the Evia program, not miss a session, and complete all 5 weeks. Some users might require more daily sessions, more suggestions of mental imagery, or to further individualize their mental imagery for coolness (the Evia app guides you in this individualization).

A potential reason why hypnotherapy is so effective in reducing hot flashes is that the suggestions and mental imagery provided during self-hypnosis sessions are theorized to change the neural activity of the hypothalamus, which is responsible for regulating core body temperature. This could explain why hypnotherapy is the only nonpharmacological treatment with notable physiologically measured hot flash reductions and why everyone, regardless of their ability to respond to hypnotic suggestions, benefits from the intervention. You can get more information and access to one free week to try the Evia app at: eviamenopause.com.

Summary

Menopause can be a stressful and overwhelming time for many women. Menopause can occur naturally (around age 52) or as a result of treatment for breast cancer or surgical removal of ovaries. Among the most distressing symptoms are menopausal hot flashes and sleep disturbances. Hypnotherapy is especially effective in relieving menopausal symptoms by reducing the frequency, severity, and bother of hot flashes, as well as by improving sleep, quality of life, and anxiety in menopausal women and breast cancer survivors. Unlike pharmacological treatment options (HRT, antidepressants, etc.), there are few or no adverse effects associated with hypnosis. Research has shown that anyone can benefit from hypnotherapy and the Evia app is a useful tool to begin using self-hypnosis to manage hot flashes.

REFERENCES

Bansal, R., & Aggarwal, N. (2019). Menopausal hot flashes: A concise review. *Journal of Mid-Life Health, 10*(1), 6-13. https://doi.org/10.4103/jmh.JMH_7_19

Barton, D. L., Schroeder, K. C. F., Banerjee, T., Wolf, S., Keith, T. Z., & Elkins, G. (2017). Efficacy of a biobehavioral intervention for hot flashes: A randomized controlled pilot study. *Menopause, 24*(7), 774-782. https://doi.org/10.1097/gme.0000000000000837

Chang, H. Y., Jotwani, A. C., Lai, Y. H., Jensen, M. P., Syrjala, K. L., Fann, J. R., & Gralow, J. (2016). Hot flashes in breast cancer survivors: Frequency, severity and impact. *The Breast, 27,* 116-121. https://doi.org/10.1016/j.breast.2016.02.013

Elkins, G. R., Fisher, W. I., Johnson, A. K., Carpenter, J. S., & Keith, T. Z. (2013). Clinical hypnosis in the treatment of postmenopausal hot flashes: A randomized controlled trial. *Menopause, 20*(3), 291-298. https://doi.org/10.1097/gme.0b013e31826ce3ed

Elkins, G., Marcus, J., Stearns, V., Perfect, M., Rajab, M. H., Ruud, C., Palamara, L., & Keith, T. (2008). Randomized trial of a hypnosis intervention for treatment of hot flashes among breast cancer survivors. *Journal of Clinical Oncology, 26*(31), 5022-5026. https://doi.org/10.1200/JCO.2008.16.6389

Elkins, G., Mosca, Y. (2017). Menopause—hot flashes. In G. R. Elkins (Ed.), *Handbook of medical and psychological hypnosis: Foundations, applications, and professional issues.* (pp. 311-315) Springer Publishing Co.

Lavigne, J. E., Heckler, C., Mathews, J. L., Palesh, O., Kirshner, J. J., Lord, R., Jacobs, A., Amos, E., Morrow, G. R., & Mustian, K. (2012). A randomized, controlled, double-blinded clinical trial of gabapentin 300 versus 900 mg versus placebo for anxiety symptoms in breast cancer survivors. *Breast Cancer Research and Treatment, 136*(2), 479–486. https://doi.org/10.1007/s10549-012-2251-x

Loibl, S., Schwedler, K., Von Minckwitz, G., Strohmeier, R., Mehta, K. M., & Kaufmann, M. (2005). Clonidine vs. venlafaxine as treatment for hot flashes in breast cancer patients: A double-blind randomised study. *Journal of Clinical Oncology, 23*(16), 8038-8038. https://doi.org/10.1200/jco.2005.23.16_suppl.8038

Maclaughlan David, S., Salzillo, S., Bowe, P., Scuncio, S., Malit, B., Raker, C., Gass, J. S., Granai, C. O., & Dizon, D. S. (2013). Randomised controlled trial comparing hypnotherapy versus gabapentin for the treatment of hot flashes in breast cancer survivors: A pilot study. *BMJ Open, 3*(9). https://doi.org/10.1136/bmjopen-2013-003138

Manson, J. E., Chlebowski, R. T., Stefanick, M. L., Aragaki, A. K., Rossouw, J. E., Prentice, R. L., Anderson, G., Howard, B. V., Thomson, C. A., LaCroix, A. Z., Wactawski-Wende, J, Jackson, R. D., Limacher, M., Margolis, K. L., Wassertheil-Smoller, S., Beresford, S. A., Cauley, J. A., Eaton, C. B., Gass, M., ... & Wallace, R. B. (2013). Menopausal hormone therapy and health outcomes during the intervention and extended poststopping phases of the Women's Health Initiative randomized trials. *JAMA, 310*(13), 1353-1368. https://doi.org/10.1001/jama.2013.278040

Muñiz V., Padilla V. J., Alldredge C. T., Elkins G. (in press). Clinical Hypnosis and Cognitive Behavioral Therapy for Hot Flashes: A Scoping Review. *Women's Health Reports.*

Posadzki, P., Lee, M. S., Moon, T. W., Choi, T. Y., Park, T. Y., & Ernst, E. (2013). Prevalence of complementary and alternative medicine (CAM) use by menopausal women: a systematic review of surveys. *Maturitas, 75*(1), 34–43. https://doi.org/10.1016/j.maturitas.2013.02.005

Rani, P., Zehra, D., Mansoor, M., & Rani, P. (2024). FDA approved fezolinetant (Veozah): a critical evaluation of its efficacy and safety for menopausal vasomotor symptoms, calling for prospective research. *Archives of Women's Mental Health*, 1-4. https://doi.org/10.1007/s00737-024-01456-y

The North American Menopause Society Advisory Panel (2023). The 2023 nonhormone therapy position statement of The North American Menopause Society. *Menopause (New York, N.Y.), 30*(6), 573–590.

Chapter 10
Sleep and Insomnia

GARY ELKINS

CAMERON ALLDREDGE

Sleep is essential for our everyday functioning and wellbeing. Unfortunately, poor sleep and insomnia are pervasive in the adult population in the United States. In fact, estimates are that 40%–45% of adults suffer from sleep disturbance. The impact of poor sleep is much more than just missing a few hours of sleep and feeling tired the next day. Sleep problems have been associated with an increased risk of cardiovascular disease, diabetes, traffic accidents, depression, and dementia. Poor sleep also occurs when dealing with health conditions and can adversely affect interpersonal relationships as well as functioning at work and home.

As we age, sleep problems become even more common. People 40 years of age or older are much more likely to have sleep difficulties. There can be many reasons for the association of poor sleep with age. The adult demands and stresses of work, financial responsibilities, care for children (even adult children), interpersonal relationship conflicts, being a caregiver for someone with dementia or disability, worry about the future, and difficulty relaxing can all contribute to poor sleep.

To determine if you have poor sleep, it is helpful to consider the signs of sleep disturbances. These include:

1. Difficulty going to sleep (i.e., it takes longer than 30 minutes to fall asleep).
2. Frequent awakenings during sleep.
3. Daytime sleepiness.
4. Fatigue.
5. Poor concentration.
6. Irritability.
7. Anxiety about sleep.
8. Feeling that you do not get enough sleep.

If you have some or most of these concerns, you likely are not getting adequate sleep.

Case Example – Martha

Martha is a 52-year-old married woman with concerns about her sleep quality. She remembers generally getting good sleep as a child and adolescent, although she sometimes had difficulty getting up and preferred to sleep longer. After graduating from high school, she attended college with an interest in teaching. At age 28, she met her husband, and they were married the following year. Martha began to have difficulty with sleep around age 35. At the time, she had two young children and was teaching at an elementary school. She stated that when trying to go to sleep, she found herself ruminating about the day ahead and found it difficult to relax. Her sleep problems have gotten worse over the past 20 years and now she has problems both going to sleep and staying asleep at night. Her usual routine is to get into bed and watch television with her husband until she feels sleepy. However, that usually doesn't happen until around 11:00 PM each night. Once she turns off the lights, she cannot fall asleep easily which leads her to feel tired when she has to wake up at 6:30 AM to begin her day. She states that she seems to get her best sleep in the early morning hours, yet that is when she has to get up.

CHAPTER 10: SLEEP AND INSOMNIA

In the past five years, she began taking sleeping pills to help her go to sleep. However, she has concerns about dependency and side effects of these medications, and they seem to be working less effectively over the past couple of years. She has tried to implement better sleep hygiene but still has poor sleep. She heard about using hypnotherapy to improve her sleep from her physician assistant and she decided to try it—we'll return to hear more about her hypnotherapy later in this chapter.

Sleep Stages

As noted in the case of Martha, she reported difficulty falling asleep and that her best sleep seemed to be in the early morning hours. To understand what might be going on, it is important to be familiar with the stages of sleep and when they occur. Sleep is divided into several stages that we cycle through multiple times each night.

> ***Stage 1*** sleep is the lightest stage of sleep which is considered the transition phase between being awake and being asleep. It is the first stage of sleep, but it does not provide good, restorative sleep. Stage 1 only makes up about 5% of sleep.
>
> ***Stage 2*** sleep is the onset of "true sleep" and involves a decrease in body temperature and heart rate where the body is more subdued and brain activity slows down. The majority of an adult's sleep is in this stage—about 45%.
>
> ***Stage 3*** sleep is characterized by deep, slow brain waves. Stage 3 sleep is important for physical recovery, and it plays a key role in growth and development. About 12% of sleep occurs in Stage 3.
>
> ***Stage 4*** (or sometimes referred to as *deep sleep*, *delta sleep*, or *slow-wave sleep*) is characterized by the presence of delta waves in the brain. It is the most restorative stage of sleep. This

stage of sleep lasts about 30 minutes at a time and about 13% of sleep in adults is comprised of Stage 4 sleep. It is the most satisfying sleep stage and occurs last or in the early morning hours. This is the type of sleep that Martha lacks most.

Rapid Eye Movement (REM) is another type of sleep that occurs several times during the sleep cycle. REM sleep is the type of sleep a person is in when they are dreaming, and it gets its name from the fact that the eyes often make rapid movements while the eyelids are closed and the body is in a state of paralysis to keep the person from acting out their dreams. REM sleep stimulates areas of the brain associated with learning and it is important for memory and problem-solving. For adults, about 25% of total sleep is spent in REM sleep.

It is most important to get sufficient deep sleep (stages 3 and 4) and REM sleep. These sleep stages provide the most restoration and are essential for helping us feel well-rested and experience good quality sleep.

Medications (Sleeping Pills)

In the case of Martha, it was noted that she had tried sleeping pills. Conventional treatment for sleep disturbances usually involves the use of sedative medications. Zolpidem (Ambien), zaleplon (Sonata), and Xanax are among the most commonly prescribed medications for sleep. These types of sedative medications may suppress REM sleep, have a negative impact on breathing well during sleep, and have a high risk of developing physical dependence. Antidepressant medications such as Trazadone and Paxil are also often prescribed for sleep. Antidepressant medications have advantages over sedative medications in that they do not carry the same high risk for abuse; however, they may also suppress REM sleep. Overall, long-term use of sleeping pills can have negative side effects, risk of dependence, and limited benefits over time. These are serious concerns, and the long-term use of these medications is generally not recommended. Therefore, as was the case with Martha, many people are encouraged to seek alternatives such as behavioral therapy and hypnotherapy to get better sleep.

Sleep Hygiene

Good sleep habits are a part of most non-pharmacological interventions for sleep. Poor habits such as excessive daytime naps, drinking caffeine late in the day, staying in bed while "tossing and turning," and engaging in stimulating activities right before bedtime can all interfere with sleep. Sleep hygiene recommendations alone are not generally sufficient to improve sleep but are foundational to improving sleep when combined with hypnotherapy. In the case of Martha, she was given the following sleep hygiene recommendations:

1. Establish a regular sleep schedule—go to bed and get up at approximately the same time each day.
2. Go to bed only when feeling drowsy and ready for sleep.
3. Don't take too many long day-time naps.
4. Avoid drinking excessive alcohol before bedtime.
5. Do not consume caffeine within 6–8 hours before bedtime.
6. Engage in light to moderate regular exercise.
7. Have a light snack before bedtime.
8. Make the room cool and dark.
9. Do not engage in stimulating activities right before sleep, especially while in bed.
10. Practice relaxing.

What the Science Says about Hypnosis for Sleep

When paired with good sleep hygiene, hypnosis has been found to be an excellent intervention to treat insomnia and improve people's sleep quality.

A recently published review article looked at 44 different studies that examined the use of hypnosis for improving sleep. The researchers found that over 70% of the studies showed that hypnosis significantly improved sleep. Specifically, the studies found hypnosis to improve sleep quantity, sleep quality, and sleep efficiency while others found hypnosis to reduce insomnia symptoms, time to fall asleep, and the number of awakenings.

A recent study of hypnosis for sleep improvement in postmenopausal women evaluated the use of self-hypnosis for sleep. Sleep was measured by sleep diaries and objectively determined by a physical device called an *actigraph*. Actigraphy involves wearing a watch-like device on the wrist that measures movement. It is a very accurate measure of sleep onset and duration. The study also involved a measurement of overall sleep quality. Sixty women were enrolled in the study and measured their sleep for eight weeks. The hypnosis intervention involved learning self-hypnosis and nightly use of hypnosis audio recordings designed for deeper sleep. The results showed a clinically meaningful improvement in sleep was achieved across all measures. Sleep measured by the actigraphy device and sleep diaries showed significant improvement. Moreover, overall sleep quality significantly improved and there was a very high degree of treatment satisfaction. Participants rated the hypnosis program as very easy to use.

Other researchers have conducted multiple studies on the use of hypnosis to increase the amount of slow wave sleep (remember, that's the kind of sleep you want more of) a person has during a nap in the middle of the day. In one of these studies, the hypnosis intervention involved listening to a hypnotic induction and mental imagery for deeper sleep (such as imagining a dolphin swim deep into the ocean) before going to sleep. They found that, with the use of hypnosis, the amount of slow wave sleep nearly doubled in both young and older participants.

How does Hypnotherapy Work to Improve Sleep?

To gain insight into how hypnotherapy works to improve sleep, we conducted a study involving 22 college students who had poor sleep. We gave them a hypnosis treatment that lasted three weeks and had their sleep measured by an actigraphy device they wore on their wrist. We found that the hypnotherapy significantly improved their sleep quality and cut the average amount of time it took them to fall asleep ***in half*** (from 28 minutes to 14 minutes, to be exact). We also looked at changes in variables typically linked to poor sleep such as rumination, worry, stress, and pre-sleep arousal. We found that our hypnosis intervention significantly helped with reducing pre-sleep arousal (especially the type associated with thinking), rumination (specifically brooding), and worry. Based on these findings, we assume that hypnosis can target core issues that prevent sleep because of its ability to help people relax both physically *and* mentally. It seems that mental relaxation and tranquility were key to improved sleep.

One of the neat advantages that hypnosis has over other psychological interventions is that it can be used right at bedtime. More than half of the 44 hypnosis studies mentioned previously used some sort of at-home practice of hypnosis with an audio recording. This means that a clinician can record a hypnotic induction and helpful suggestions for sleep for a person to listen to while they are in bed and ready to sleep. The hypnosis recording can contain hypnotic suggestions designed to help someone reach a physical and mental state that allows for restful sleep.

Hypnotherapy for Sleep

Before beginning to use hypnosis for sleep, it may be important to determine what type of sleep problem you are experiencing. There are a number of disorders that can affect sleep such as sleep apnea (a condition where breathing is interrupted or stops briefly during sleep), depression (depression can be associated with too much or too little sleep), sleep movement disorders (sleepwalking, REM sleep disorders), nightmare disorder (can be associated with post-traumatic stress), and other sleep disorders. It is advised to seek medical consultation for assessment and guidance on interventions. This may involve a review of symptoms, history, or an individualized sleep study. Many individuals also benefit from follow-up with a health care provider with expertise in sleep.

A review of the recommendations for sleep hygiene can also be helpful. It is important to have the right environment for good sleep and healthy sleep behaviors. With these things in mind, most individuals find that self-hypnosis is easy to use, exceptionally helpful for relaxation, decreases worry and rumination, and leads to deeper sleep.

Usually, individuals are asked to listen to a hypnosis recording when they get into bed, turn the lights off, and are ready to go to sleep. It can be very helpful to listen to the self-hypnosis audio recordings using headphones or ear buds with the volume set rather low so that it is easy to drift off to sleep. The hypnosis sessions usually involve a hypnotic induction with suggestions for relaxation and "letting go" of tension and stress. This is followed by suggestions for deepening the hypnotic state and then suggestions for deeper sleep, positive dreams, and ease in going back to sleep if awakenings occur. Most people use self-hypnosis on a nightly basis and find it to be very pleasant. There are many resources that provide information on hypnosis and sleep. Mindset Health (mindsethealth.com) is an example of an excellent resource.

How Martha Used Hypnotherapy to Improve Sleep

With this information about hypnotherapy for sleep, we return to the case of Martha and how she used hypnosis to improve her sleep. Martha is a real person who participated in one of our clinical hypnosis studies. At the start of the study, Martha was only getting an average of about 5 hours of sleep per night. She was screened for other sleep disorders and depression. She was also given information on good sleep hygiene and set a regular time to go to bed at night and to get up each morning. She was already exercising by walking after work each day. Martha was introduced to hypnotherapy by a discussion about hypnosis and how it can improve the duration and quality of sleep. She was given an opportunity to ask questions and then invited to experience a hypnotic induction for deep relaxation and post-hypnotic suggestions for going to sleep more quickly, getting more sleep, and having deeper sleep. She found the hypnotic induction to be very relaxing and her confidence in being able to use self-hypnosis increased. At the end of the session, she was provided access to hypnosis audio recordings that she would use each night for the next 2 months. During this time, she maintained daily sleep diaries and completed a questionnaire about her sleep quality.

Examples of the hypnotic suggestions that were included in the audio recordings are:

> *"As you become very deeply relaxed ... every muscle and every fiber of your body, deeply relaxed ... no tension ... no stress ... you can enter an even deeper level of hypnosis ... going deeper and deeper into this hypnotic state ... .any worries and any concerns can be set aside ... as you allow yourself to drift ... letting go ... more relaxed ... and soon you can see a path before you ... a pleasant mountain path ... It can be pleasant to be in a peaceful place in the mountains ... and to walk down a path to your cabin in the mountains ... It is a day when the air is cool and you may notice a few snowflakes as you walk down this path. Every step you take, takes you deeper into this hypnotic state and toward good, deep sleep ... You might be aware of your breathing ... and each breath allows you to relax even more ... as I count from 1 to 10, experiencing all of the coolness and calmness of this place and each number takes you deeper into this hypnotic state ... so that you can see the cabin up ahead ... 1 ... 2 ... 3 ... 4 ... 5 ... 6 ... 7 ... 8 ... 9 ... 10. Now you are there and as you go into the cabin, feeling safe and secure ... a place and a time where you can lay down on a comfortable bed and drift into deep sleep ... effortlessly ... and outside the cabin the snowflakes fall from way up high in the clouds ... they drift down ... down ... down ... past the clouds, the tops of the trees ... and all the way down ... and so you can drift all the way down into deep slow wave sleep ... good sleep, restful sleep...the sleep you need ... "*

By the end of the fifth week, Martha was sleeping much better. Her sleep diaries revealed she was going to sleep within 15 minutes on average and getting 7 ½ hours of sleep per night. She was very pleased and continued using the audio recordings and self-hypnosis. After eight weeks, her sleep had improved even more and her overall sleep quality had improved by over 50%, reflecting more slow wave sleep.

Summary

The existing research demonstrates hypnotherapy can be very effective in increasing both the amount of sleep as well as the quality of sleep, evidenced by deeper, more satisfying sleep. While it usually works best when combined with good sleep hygiene and the guidance of a healthcare provider, it can be self-administered and used effectively when indicated. Practicing with an audio recording is advantageous because it can be used at night when a person is ready to go to sleep. I (GE) personally have used self-hypnosis for years to manage stress, increase mindfulness, and have good sleep most nights! I (CA) have also personally used self-hypnosis to help fall asleep and have seen it make an immense difference in the lives of others who struggle with sleep.

REFERENCES

Alldredge, C., Snyder, M., Stork, S., & Elkins, G. (2024). Exploring variables associated with the effects of a self-administered hypnosis intervention for improving sleep quality. *International Journal of Clinical and Experimental Hypnosis, 72(2),* 94-108. https://doi.org/10.1080/00207144.2023.2278720

Chamine, I., Atchley, R., & Oken, B. (2018). Hypnosis intervention effects on sleep outcomes: A systematic review. *Journal of Clinical Sleep Medicine, 14(3),* 271-283. https://doi.org/10.5664/jcsm.6952

Cordi, M.J., Hirsiger, S., Merillat, S., & Rasch, B. (2015). Improving sleep and cognition by hypnotic suggestion in the elderly. *Neuropsychologia, 69,* 176–182. https://doi.org/10.1016/j.neuropsychologia.2015.02.001

Elkins, G. (2014). *Hypnotic relaxation therapy: Principles and applications.* Springer Publishing Co.

Cordi, M., Rasch, B. (2017). Increasing slow-wave sleep by hypnotic suggestions. In G. R. Elkins (Ed.), *Handbook of medical and psychological hypnosis: Foundations, applications, and professional issues.* (pp.611-620). Springer Publishing Co.

Elkins, G. (2022). *Introduction to clinical hypnosis: The basics and beyond.* Mountain Pine Publishing.

Elkins, G., Otte, J., Carpenter, J., Roberts, L., Jackson, L., Kekecs, Z., Patterson, V., & Keith, T. (2021). Hypnosis intervention for sleep disturbance: Determination of optimal dose and method of delivery for postmenopausal women. *International Journal of Clinical and Experimental Hypnosis, 69(3)*, 323-345. https://doi.org/10.1080/00207144.2021.1919520

Morin, C., & Benca, R. (2012). Chronic insomnia. *Lancet, 379-(9821),* 1129-1141.

Wofford, N., Snyder, M., Corlett, C. & Elkins, G. (2023). Systematic review of hypnotherapy for sleep and sleep disturbance. *International Journal of Clinical and Experimental Hypnosis, 71(3),* 176-215. https://doi.org/10.1080/00207144.2023.2226177

Chapter 11
Trauma and PTSD

Skyla Renner-Wilms
Cameron Alldredge

Most individuals either witness or directly experience at least one highly distressing and/or life-altering event at some point in their lifetime. Such events may include experiencing natural disasters, severe illness, vehicle collisions, violence, military combat, or abuse. These types of experiences are commonly labeled as *trauma*. While not all individuals who experience a traumatic event go on to develop post-traumatic stress disorder (PTSD), about 6% of American adults will have PTSD at some point in their lives. Among the various treatment options available, hypnotherapy has proven to be effective in addressing both the physical and emotional responses associated with trauma and PTSD.

PTSD Symptom Categories

PTSD symptoms are divided into four main categories: re-experiencing, avoidance, negative alterations in thoughts and mood, and changes in physical and emotional responses. Here's a closer look at each category.

> ***Re-experiencing*** symptoms include intrusive—or unwanted—thoughts about the traumatic event. Sometimes individuals may feel as though they are suddenly reliving the trauma, which is often referred to as a "flashback." This group of symptoms also

includes upsetting dreams about the event and experiencing severe distress when reminded of the event. Often, individuals may encounter a "cue" or "trigger" that reminds them of the event, such as hearing a familiar sound associated with the event (e.g., gunfire, fireworks) and/or seeing a similar location to where the event occurred (e.g., location of a car accident); encountering the trigger may result in the person experiencing heightened emotional and physical responses.

Avoidance symptoms include a person's efforts to avoid memories, thoughts, and feelings associated with the traumatic event. This often expands to include avoiding people, places, objects, situations, or activities that remind a person of the event. Avoidance can also involve an outright refusal to talk about the event with others or allow themselves to think about it.

Negative alterations in thoughts and mood involve negative thoughts about oneself, others, or the world because of the traumatic experience. This may also include feeling hopeless about the future, distancing oneself from others, and/or feeling emotionally numb. People who have experienced trauma may have difficulty connecting with others and engaging in activities they once enjoyed. This category also includes memory problems related to a traumatic event. Often, when attempting to recall the event, an individual may experience significant gaps in their memory.

Changes in physical and emotional responses include being easily startled or constantly on guard. Such responses may also involve difficulties sleeping, concentrating, and managing anger. Following a traumatic event, people may engage in self-destructive behavior to cope, such as substance use or risky sexual activity. This category also includes a person's overwhelming feelings of guilt and shame associated with a traumatic event.

Psychological Treatments for PTSD

There are a variety of therapies that are *trauma-focused*, which means they tackle trauma directly by addressing its emotional, cognitive, and physical aspects. A common theme among treatments used for PTSD is an element of "exposure" which typically involves repeatedly revisiting and verbally recounting the traumatic event in a controlled setting to reduce its emotional impact. There's also an element of helping individuals understand and change how they think about the trauma and its aftermath. Activities may involve talking through the trauma, writing about it, and challenging unhelpful thoughts to reduce PTSD symptoms.

A common issue with trauma-focused treatment is *dropout*, and the dropout rates seem to be similar across the different therapy modalities. Patients may prematurely leave trauma-focused therapy for a range of reasons including high emotional distress, excessive fear, or a lack of noticeable improvement. These factors contribute to an average dropout rate of around 21% and create a barrier for individuals seeking relief from PTSD-related symptoms.

Research on Hypnotherapy for PTSD and Trauma

Past research has shown that hypnotherapy can significantly reduce PTSD symptoms, regardless of how long ago the trauma happened or whether it was witnessed or directly experienced. Specifically, it has been found that hypnotherapy effectively targets symptoms of intrusion (i.e., unwanted memories) and avoidance (i.e., going out of one's way to not be confronted with the trauma). Self-hypnosis has been found to help individuals effectively manage and reduce intrusive and unwanted memories or flashbacks. Additionally, some studies have found that hypnosis is effective in reducing PTSD symptoms in children and adolescents. Hypnosis can also be used to supplement other commonly used trauma treatments, such as cognitive-behavioral therapy (CBT) and prolonged exposure (PE).

How Hypnotherapy Addresses Trauma

Hypnosis treats trauma by facilitating a safe environment where traumatic memories can be accessed and reframed. In this context, *reframing* refers to changing the way a person thinks about their traumatic event to alter its emotional impact on them. An example of reframing in hypnotherapy is helping a person experience what it might be like for their adult-self to comfort their child-self at the end of a painful memory involving childhood trauma. Another example is using hypnosis to help someone explore and experience an alternative ending to their traumatic event—usually something they deeply wish would have happened in the moment. Like other techniques, there is still an element of exposure to the traumatic memory, but the context of hypnosis makes it more manageable and less distressing compared to other methods.

Moreover, hypnotherapy can promote a sense of *dual awareness* where individuals are simultaneously aware of both the present moment and the traumatic memory. As a result, a person is reminded that the trauma or distressing event is in the past and they are safe in the current moment. When a person feels safe, power is taken away from the traumatic memory and given to the individual. That increased sense of power manifests itself as an improved ability to manage difficult memories and decrease responses to external triggers. Hypnotherapy sessions will also often include elements of direct empowerment with hypnotic suggestions designed to improve a person's perspective of themselves, their future, and the world around them.

Case Example – Andrew

Andrew was a patient of mine (CA) who sought therapy with me while he was in his mid-20s due to intimacy issues with his wife along with severe symptoms of anxiety and depression. He became interested in trying hypnotherapy to help him with traumatic, early childhood sexual abuse that he experienced from a babysitter. In conjunction with another trauma-informed approach, we decided to use hypnosis for exposure exercises.

Andrew was highly hypnotizable and could vividly re-experience the traumatic events. At first, he experienced these memories as if he was an outside observer. Gradually, as he felt the memories were more manageable, he allowed himself to experience them as if they were happening firsthand. From there, we completed an exercise where he experienced an alternate ending to a traumatic memory. He hated the feeling of being so young and powerless during the disturbing events, so he assumed he would want the alternate ending to involve having superhuman strength and being able to "beat up" the babysitter. What actually happened during the hypnosis, however, was very different and insightful. He simply wanted his mother to come home early and intervene. It was a profound and healing moment for him to experience what it may have been like if that had happened.

Andrew was also guided through an experience where his adult-self was able to comfort his child-self. He imagined being in his childhood room and embracing his five-year-old-self with messages of compassion, empathy, and understanding. This helped to address a lot of the shame he felt around the event. Over time, Andrew found that his marital relationship was strengthened, his discomfort with intimacy had dissolved, and he saw a lift in his anxious and depressive symptoms.

Summary

Experiencing traumatic events can drastically impact one's quality of life. Hypnosis is an effective treatment that can be used to treat PTSD-related symptoms. Hypnotherapy creates a safe environment where memories of trauma, which people often avoid or keep hidden, can be brought to the surface and processed in a helpful way. Hypnosis allows individuals to confront and process difficult memories in a manner that is productive and controlled without getting too overwhelmed. Hypnotherapy also facilitates an improved sense of safety and empowerment for individuals who have experienced a traumatic event.

REFERENCES

Bremer-Hoeve, S., van Vliet, N. I., van Bronswijk, S. C., Huntjens, R. J., de Jongh, A., & van Dijk, M. K. (2023). Predictors of treatment dropout in patients with posttraumatic stress disorder due to childhood abuse. *Frontiers in Psychiatry*, *14*, 1194669. https://doi.org/10.3389/fpsyt.2023.1194669

Christensen, C. (2017). Posttraumatic stress disorder. In G. R. Elkins (Ed.), *Handbook of medical and psychological hypnosis: Foundations, applications, and professional issues* (pp. 599–604). Springer Publishing Company.

Hembree, E. A., Foa, E. B., Dorfan, N. M., Street, G. P., Kowalski, J., & Tu, X. (2003). Do patients drop out prematurely from exposure therapy for PTSD?. *Journal of Traumatic Stress*, *16*(6), 555–562. https://doi.org/10.1023/B:JOTS.0000004078.93012.7d

Hembree, E. A., Rauch, S. A. M., & Foa, E. B. (2003). Beyond the manual: The insider's guide to prolonged exposure therapy for PTSD. *Cognitive and Behavioral Practice*, *10*(1), 22–30. https://doi.org/10.1016/S1077-7229(03)80005-6

O'Toole, S. K., Solomon, S. L., & Bergdahl, S. A. (2016). A meta-analysis of hypnotherapeutic techniques in the treatment of PTSD symptoms. *Journal of Traumatic Stress*, *29*(1), 97–100. https://doi.org/10.1002/jts.22077

Rotaru, T. Ștefan, & Rusu, A. (2015). A meta-analysis for the efficacy of hypnotherapy in alleviating PTSD symptoms. *International Journal of Clinical and Experimental Hypnosis*, *64*(1), 116–136. https://doi.org/10.1080/00207144.2015.1099406

Spiegel, D., & Cardena, E. (1990). New uses of hypnosis in the treatment of posttraumatic stress disorder. *The Journal of Clinical Psychiatry*, *51 Suppl*, 39–46.

Watkins, L. E., Sprang, K. R., & Rothbaum, B. O. (2018). Treating PTSD: A review of evidence-based psychotherapy interventions. *Frontiers in Behavioral Neuroscience*, *12*, 258. https://doi.org/10.3389/fnbeh.2018.00258

Youn, S. J., Mackintosh, M. A., Wiltsey Stirman, S., Patrick, K. A., Aguilar Silvan, Y., Bartuska, A. D., Shtasel, D. L., & Marques, L. (2019). Client-level predictors of treatment engagement, outcome and dropout: Moving beyond demographics. *General Psychiatry*, *32*(6), e100153. https://doi.org/10.1136/gpsych-2019-100153

Chapter 12
Irritable Bowel Syndrome

Vanessa Muñiz
Cameron Alldredge

With an estimated prevalence of 11% of adults worldwide—more than 102 million people—irritable bowel syndrome (IBS) is one of the most common gut-related disorders. IBS is described as "a disorder of the gut-brain interaction," in which a person might experience "recurrent abdominal pain and altered bowel movements in the form of diarrhea, constipation, or alternating between the two." Severe IBS symptoms are associated with significant impairment in work, regular activity, social life, and general wellbeing.

IBS is prevalent across all age groups; however, over half of all IBS patients experience their first occurrence of symptoms before age 35, and IBS prevalence is lower in patients over 50 years as compared to those who are younger. Moreover, women are up to two times more likely to experience IBS throughout their lifetime than men, and it is believed that women may experience more severe symptoms and daily interference caused by IBS symptoms compared to men. In attempts to better understand patient experiences with IBS, one study revealed that a common concern, and stereotype, among men suffering from IBS is the incorrect notion that this condition is a "female health concern."

IBS Symptoms

While core IBS symptoms commonly change over time, chronic IBS symptoms might persist for up to 10 years in many individuals. However, several qualitative studies and validated measures have provided insight into the average symptom patterns and warning signs that one should look out for. For example, in the first three months following diagnosis, patients might experience an average of four distinct symptom episodes (commonly referred to as "flare-ups") per month. The duration and intervals of these episodes tend to differ from person to person. Potential gastrointestinal (GI) symptoms present during these flare-ups include abdominal pain, changes in bowel habits (such as diarrhea, constipation, or a mix of the two), bloating, flatulence, and abdominal distension.

Causes & Risk Factors of IBS

IBS is not caused by one specific thing. Instead, IBS tends to originate from a combination of different factors that may impact different people. Some of these include:

- A family history of IBS
- Disturbances in intestinal bacterial colonization (such as a change in the type of bacteria or bacterial overgrowth in the small intestine)
- Stressful or traumatic events in childhood (e.g., physical or sexual abuse)
- Food intolerances or sensitivities as well as irregular or improper eating habits

Having any of these risk factors does not mean you have or will develop IBS, but they are good indicators that you are at higher risk of developing IBS. Although some symptoms typically have a physical manifestation, a history of mental health issues, such as depression, anxiety, or somatic symptom disorder, might also place individuals at higher risk for IBS. According to several scientific studies, the majority of patients suffering from IBS symptoms believe the primary triggers for their symptoms are related to poor diet and chronic stress.

Hypnotherapy for IBS

Fortunately, clinical hypnosis has demonstrated encouraging and consistent effectiveness in improving IBS symptoms in numerous clinical trials. Hypnosis for the treatment of IBS is referred to as *gut-directed hypnotherapy* in scientific research and has been studied since the early 1980s. According to a systematic review combining over 460 participants receiving gut-directed hypnotherapy, those assigned to the hypnosis treatment saw a significantly greater reduction in their short-term GI symptoms when compared to conventional treatment or low-FODMAP-foods diet, and a reduction of over 50% in their long-term symptoms when compared to placebo, waitlist, or psychoeducation control groups.

Similar findings are shown in research on gut-directed hypnotherapy with significant reductions in IBS symptoms found among studies in both specialized research centers and hospital settings. In fact, a randomized controlled trial assessing the efficacy of gut-directed hypnotherapy in 138 participants across two different hospitals found a significantly greater reduction in IBS-related symptom severity among participants in the hypnotherapy treatment compared to a supportive therapy control group. These improvements in GI symptoms were maintained for 42% of the participants at one-year follow-up, and for 28% after two years.

One large study compared the results of participants assigned to low-FODMAP diet only, gut-directed hypnotherapy-treatment only, or a combination of the two. The results showed that participants experienced significant improvements across all three treatment groups. More specifically, 71% of low-FODMAP diet-only participants, 72% of gut-directed hypnotherapy-only participants, and 72% of combined hypnotherapy and low-FODMAP participants reported significant improvements that lasted through 6-month follow-up. It is important to note that the greatest improvements in anxiety and depression were reported by the participants receiving only gut-directed hypnotherapy.

Primarily, as you may have already gathered from the results mentioned in these studies, the main goals for gut-directed hypnotherapy are to achieve a substantial reduction in the frequency and intensity of pain, discomfort, and stress caused by IBS symptoms, strengthen one's control over gut function, normalize bowel activity, decrease one's reactivity of their GI tract in response to life stressors, and improve overall physical well-being and calm the gut. To achieve this, hypnotic suggestions for improving gut control might sound like this:

> *"...as you practice these skills, you will feel more and more confident in your ability to control your gut, and you experience an increased ability to do more of the things you enjoy... feeling much more able to control your gut whenever you would like to."*

Case Example – Kimber

Kimber was a 28-year-old female diagnosed with irritable bowel syndrome. She underwent diagnostic tests, such as a colonoscopy, and was specifically diagnosed by her gastroenterologist with irritable bowel syndrome with predominant diarrhea (IBS-D). Her symptoms included bloating, abdominal discomfort, loose stools, and frequent diarrhea. Her symptoms started around age 19 when she started attending college. Kimber noticed that her symptoms were worse after eating fatty foods and when she was stressed.

Kimber worked as a nurse and was in a romantic relationship. She missed several days of work each quarter due to excessive IBS symptoms and her symptoms always seemed to flare up after an argument with her partner. After trying to change her diet and only seeing minimal improvement, she decided to try alternative approaches for managing her IBS symptoms and stress. In her search for a solution, Kimber read that hypnotherapy is a recommended treatment and decided to try it, despite some initial skepticism.

Kimber found a clinician trained in hypnotherapy whom she met with virtually for 10 sessions. The initial sessions provided her with accurate information about hypnosis and gave her an idea of how clinical hypnosis works to treat IBS. She kept a daily record of her symptoms and identified that stress and certain foods trigger her IBS symptoms. The FODMAP diet was recommended to her, and hypnotherapy sessions focused on helping facilitate relaxation and peace, as well as experiencing a "calm gut." She was provided with audio recordings to practice with on her own, which she listened to daily. After 10 sessions, Kimber's IBS symptoms were so minimal that she often forgot about them, and she also felt an increased ability to manage stress.

Digital Hypnotherapy for Irritable Bowel Syndrome

Given that the majority of individuals experiencing IBS report mild symptoms most of the time, only 30% of those experiencing IBS seek medical attention for symptom reduction and management of IBS. Unfortunately, it is common that only individuals experiencing severe and highly disruptive IBS symptoms seek healthcare services for said symptoms. The *Nerva* app is a mobile-health application that provides a gut-directed hypnotherapy program designed and developed in collaboration with Dr. Simone Peters based on her research from Monash University. Nerva offers a 6-week-long intervention with 42 brief hypnotherapy sessions (one per day) that have been tested in previous clinical trials. The Nerva app also offers two resources in addition to the audio sessions: informational readings and deep-breathing exercises. Past studies support the app's effectiveness in helping more than 70% of people with IBS significantly improve their IBS-related GI symptoms from their home.

Summary

IBS often involves uncomfortable and impairing symptoms that can negatively affect the lives of those who experience it. Hypnotherapy has been shown to help people manage IBS as well as available options and is sometimes shown to be superior to conventional treatments. Clinical hypnosis can be used to reduce the frequency and intensity of IBS-related pain and discomfort, improve one's sense of control over gut function, normalize bowel activity, and decrease stress. The mobile app, Nerva, is a helpful resource for individuals interested in trying hypnosis for IBS.

REFERENCES

Björkman, I., Dellenborg, L., Ringström, G., Simrén, M., & Jakobsson Ung, E. (2013). The gendered impact of irritable bowel syndrome: A qualitative study of patients' experiences. *Journal of Advanced Nursing*, *70*(6), 1334-1343. https://doi.org/10.1111/jan.12294

Canavan, C., West, J., & Card, T. (2014). The epidemiology of irritable bowel syndrome. *Clinical Epidemiology*, *6*, 71–80. https://doi.org/10.2147/CLEP.S40245

Casiday, R. E., Hungin, A. P., Cornford, C. S., de Wit, N. J., & Blell, M. T. (2009). Patients' explanatory models for irritable bowel syndrome: Symptoms and treatment more important than explaining aetiology. *Family Practice*, *26*(1), 40–47. https://doi.org/10.1093/fampra/cmn087

Dixon-Woods, M., & Critchley, S. (2000). Medical and lay views of irritable bowel syndrome. *Family Practice*, *17*(2), 108–113. https://doi.org/10.1093/fampra/17.2.108

Drossman, D. A., Camilleri, M., Mayer, E. A., & Whitehead, W. E. (2002). AGA technical review on irritable bowel syndrome. *Gastroenterology*, *123*(6), 2108–2131. https://doi.org/10.1053/gast.2002.37095

Drossman, D. A., Morris, C. B., Schneck, S., Hu, Y. J., Norton, N. J., Norton, W. F., Weinland, S. R., Dalton, C., Leserman, J., & Bangdiwala, S. I. (2009). International survey of patients with IBS: Symptom features and their severity, health status, treatments, and risk taking to achieve clinical benefit. *Journal of Clinical Gastroenterology*, *43*(6), 541–550. https://doi.org/10.1097/MCG.0b013e318189a7f9

Frändemark, Å., Törnblom, H., Jakobsson, S., & Simrén, M. (2018). Work productivity and activity impairment in irritable bowel syndrome (IBS): A multifaceted problem. *The American Journal of Gastroenterology*, *113*(10), 1540–1549. https://doi.org/10.1038/s41395-018-0262-x

Gonsalkorale, W. M. (2006). Gut-directed hypnotherapy: The Manchester approach for treatment of irritable bowel syndrome. *International Journal of Clinical and Experimental Hypnosis*, *54*(1), 27-50. https://doi.org/10.1080/00207140500323030

Goodoory, V. C., Ng, C. E., Black, C. J., & Ford, A. C. (2022). Impact of Rome IV irritable bowel syndrome on work and activities of daily living. *Alimentary Pharmacology & Therapeutics*, *56*(5), 844–856. https://doi.org/10.1111/apt.17132

Kim, Y. S., & Kim, N. (2018). Sex-gender differences in irritable bowel syndrome. *Journal of Neurogastroenterology and Motility*, *24*(4), 544–558. https://doi.org/10.5056/jnm18082

Lacy, B. E., Mearin, F., Chang, L., Chey, W. D., Lembo, A. J., Simren, M., & Spiller, R. (2016). Bowel disorders. *Gastroenterology*, *150*(6), 1393-1407. https://doi.org/10.1053/j.gastro.2016.02.031

Lacy, B. E., Weiser, K., Noddin, L., Robertson, D. J., Crowell, M. D., Parratt-Engstrom, C., & Grau, M. V. (2007). Irritable bowel syndrome: Patients' attitudes, concerns and level of knowledge. *Alimentary Pharmacology & Therapeutics*, *25*(11), 1329–1341. https://doi.org/10.1111/j.1365-2036.2007.03328.x

Lindfors, P., Unge, P., Arvidsson, P., Nyhlin, H., Björnsson, E., Abrahamsson, H., & Simrén, M. (2012). Effects of gut-directed hypnotherapy on IBS in different clinical settings—results from two randomized, controlled trials. *The American Journal of Gastroenterology, 107*(2), 276-285. https://doi.org/10.1038/ajg.2011.340

Longstreth, G. F., Thompson, W. G., Chey, W. D., Houghton, L. A., Mearin, F., & Spiller, R. C. (2006). Functional bowel disorders. *Gastroenterology*, *130*(5), 1480–1491. https://doi.org/10.1053/j.gastro.2005.11.061

Lovell, R. M., & Ford, A. C. (2012). Global prevalence of and risk factors for irritable bowel syndrome: A meta-analysis. *Clinical Gastroenterology and Hepatology, 10*(7), 712–721. https://doi.org/10.1016/j.cgh.2012.02.029

Maxwell, P. R., Mendall, M. A., & Kumar, D. (1997). Irritable bowel syndrome. *Lancet, 350*(9092), 1691–1695. https://doi.org/10.1016/s0140-6736(97)05276-8

Olafsdottir, L. B., Gudjonsson, H., Jonsdottir, H. H., & Thjodleifsson, B. (2010). Stability of the irritable bowel syndrome and subgroups as measured by three diagnostic criteria - a 10-year follow-up study. *Alimentary Pharmacology & Therapeutics, 32*(5), 670–680. https://doi.org/10.1111/j.1365-2036.2010.04388.x

Palsson, O.S. (2015). Hypnosis treatment of gastrointestinal disorders: A comprehensive review of the empirical evidence. *American Journal of Clinical Hypnosis, 58*(2), 134-158. https://doi.org/10.1080/00029157.2015.1039114

Palsson, O. S. (2017). Irritable bowel syndrome. In G. R. Elkins (Ed.), *Handbook of medical and psychological hypnosis: Foundations, applications, and professional issues* (pp. 283-293). Springer Publishing Company.

Palsson, O. S., & Drossman, D. A. (2005). Psychiatric and psychological dysfunction in irritable bowel syndrome and the role of psychological treatments. *Gastroenterology Clinics of North America, 34*(2), 281–303. https://doi.org/10.1016/j.gtc.2005.02.004

Palsson, O. S., & van Tilburg, M. (2015). Hypnosis and guided imagery treatment for gastrointestinal disorders: Experience with scripted protocols developed at the University of North Carolina. *American Journal of Clinical Hypnosis, 58*(1), 5-21. https://doi.org/10.1080/00029157.2015.1012705

Peters, S., Gibson, P., & Halmos, E. (2021). Mobile app-delivered gut-directed hypnotherapy significantly reduces symptoms of irritable bowel syndrome: Is this the way of the future?. *Gastroenterology, 160*(6), S-128. https://doi.org/10.1016/s0016-5085(21)01058-1

Peters, S. L., Yao, C. K., Philpott, H., Yelland, G. W., Muir, J. G., & Gibson, P. R. (2016). Randomised clinical trial: The efficacy of gut-directed hypnotherapy is similar to that of the low FODMAP diet for the treatment of irritable bowel syndrome. *Alimentary Pharmacology & Therapeutics, 44*(5), 447-459. https://doi.org/10.1111/apt.13706

Schaefert, R., Klose, P., Moser, G., & Häuser, W. (2014). Efficacy, tolerability, and safety of hypnosis in adult irritable bowel syndrome: systematic review and meta-analysis. *Psychosomatic Medicine, 76*(5), 389–398. https://doi.org/10.1097/PSY.0000000000000039

Symptoms & Causes of Irritable Bowel Syndrome—NIDDK. (n.d.). National Institute of Diabetes and Digestive and Kidney Diseases. Retrieved August 11, 2024, from https://www.niddk.nih.gov/health-information/digestive-diseases/irritable-bowel-syndrome/symptoms-causes

Trindade, I. A., Melchior, C., Törnblom, H., & Simrén, M. (2022). Quality of life in irritable bowel syndrome: Exploring mediating factors through structural equation modelling. *Journal of Psychosomatic Research*, *159*, 110809. https://doi.org/10.1016/j.jpsychores.2022.110809

Weinland, S. R., Morris, C. B., Hu, Y., Leserman, J., Bangdiwala, S. I., & Drossman, D. A. (2011). Characterization of episodes of irritable bowel syndrome using ecological momentary assessment. *The American Journal of Gastroenterology*, *106*(10), 1813–1820. https://doi.org/10.1038/ajg.2011.170

Chapter 13
Stress Management

VANESSA MUÑIZ

VICTOR JULIAN PADILLA

GARY ELKINS

A racing heart. Shallow breathing. Tense muscles. A ringing in the ears. The body has many methods of alerting you to perceived external threats. Whether these threats are physical, such as a cooking fire, or psychological, such as a work deadline, stress is an inevitable part of living. Stress can act as a driver for change and productivity when you have the resources and support needed to manage it; however, it can negatively impact your health and wellbeing if it becomes too great to handle or if it occurs over a sustained period of time. Hypnotherapy can be an effective tool for stress management. Suggestions for relaxation, mindful acceptance, and changes in how we perceive events are components of hypnosis that can help reduce and manage stress. This chapter provides the essentials of how hypnotherapy is used to manage stress in everyday life as well as more severe chronic stress.

What is Stress?

Stress is a physical and emotional response that occurs when people face challenges or demands in life. Stress is usually temporary and situation-specific. Once the stressful event is over, the stress response generally subsides. During the stress response, your body releases hormones that can cause increased heart rate, faster breathing, narrowing of blood vessels, and increased muscle tension. This reaction is often referred to as the "fight or flight response." In small amounts, stress can be motivating and help you tackle challenges. This is known as *eustress* or "good stress."

For example, Dominic, a 32-year-old software developer, recently accepted a position at a leading tech company. Although he had experience in the field, this new role came with more responsibilities, including leading a team and working on high-profile projects. The challenge was exciting. As his start date approached, Dominic felt a sense of eustress (i.e., positive stress that energized rather than overwhelmed him) and he was eager to take on the new challenges. These positive feelings motivated Dominic to prepare thoroughly. He brushed up on the latest technologies, reviewed leadership strategies, and familiarized himself with the company's products and culture. In this example, the eustress helped Dominic transition smoothly into the job, fostered professional growth and satisfaction. The positive stress of starting a new job catalyzed Dominic to thrive in his career.

On the other hand, when stress feels unmanageable or seems threatening, it can lead to feelings of overwhelm. This negative stress is known as *distress,* and it's what most of us refer to when we talk about stress. Common characteristics of distress include an increase in heart rate, blood pressure, oxygen consumption, stress hormones, and muscle tension. While eustress contributes to growth and wellbeing, distress can harm mental and physical health if it becomes chronic. For instance, chronic stress places individuals at higher risk of diabetes, peptic ulcers, and viral infections.

In Dominic's example, if the company culture is highly competitive and demands constant high performance, the ongoing pressure could wear Dominic down over time. What started as an exciting challenge could become a source of chronic stress, leading to feelings of being overwhelmed and trapped. Alternatively, if Dominic sets unrealistic expectations for himself or becomes overly concerned about making mistakes, the pressure to perform perfectly could cause his stress to shift from motivating to debilitating (i.e., from eustress to distress). Fear of failure might lead to anxiety and self-doubt. In these scenarios, the motivating stress that initially helped Dominic excel could become a source of distress, leading to decreased job satisfaction, mental and physical health issues, and potentially even burnout if not managed properly.

Prolonged distress can negatively impact every organ system, from raising stress hormone levels to causing sleep disruptions, muscle tension, metabolic issues, immune system problems, and inflammation. Chronic stress has been associated with the development of various diseases, including cardiovascular disease, diabetes, cancer, autoimmune disorders, and mental health issues like depression and anxiety. Relying on alcohol or drugs to cope with stress can worsen these effects and further disrupt sleep.

What is the Science Behind Hypnotherapy for Stress Management?

Stress management is frequently incorporated into hypnotherapy to help people achieve a state of relaxation and calmness. A recent systematic review from 2017 identified several clinical studies demonstrating the efficacy of hypnotherapy for stress management. The randomized clinical trials showed that hypnotherapy can be instrumental to achieving relaxation and improved coping. For example, a recent clinical study examined a hypnotherapy program for stress reduction and found that participants reported that the hypnotherapy sessions improved their coping abilities and increased their sense of control over stress. Significant improvements in their stress and depression scores were seen from the start to the end of treatment. Hypnotherapy for stress management has been shown to be an important component of hypnotherapy for other treatments as well, such as hypnosis for smoking cessation and for managing anxiety, sleep disturbances, and irritable bowel syndrome. According to the research, using clinical hypnosis to focus on stress relief can help lead to improvements in other symptoms and problems.

Hypnotic Induction for Stress Reduction

Hypnotherapy usually involves a series of sessions in which the individual learns how to use hypnosis for relaxation and calmness. The hypnotherapy sessions guide the individual into a deeply relaxed state using soothing language and positive visualization. While in this state, one feels more open to positive suggestions and imagery that promote relaxation and calmness. The individual is usually provided with audio recordings and instructions for self-hypnosis to help them visualize themselves handling stressful situations easily while feeling confident and in control. Techniques such as anchoring might also be used, in which the patient is more aware of the present moment and responds to guided suggestions for feeling calm and compassionate toward themself. This helps the individual achieve relaxation, view stressful events more positively, and learn to cope better with stress.

Summary

Hypnotherapy is a useful tool for those looking to manage their stress during their day-to-day lives. It is an easy-to-use technique that you can practice on your own or with the assistance of a licensed hypnotherapist or hypnotherapy app. Its low effort requirements make it an appealing option for those dealing with the stresses of everyday life as well as chronic stress. Research on the use of hypnotherapy for treating stress is promising thus far, and suggestions for stress management have been frequently incorporated into hypnotherapy treatments for many other conditions.

REFERENCES

Anderson, N. B., Bennett Johnson, S., Belar, C. D., Breckler, S. J., Nordal, K. C., Ballard, D., et al. (2012). *Stress in America: Our health at risk*. American Psychological Association.

Chamine, I., Atchley, R., & Oken, B. S. (2018). Hypnosis intervention effects on sleep outcomes: A systematic review. *Journal of Clinical Sleep Medicine, 14*(02), 271–283. https://doi.org/10.5664/jcsm.6952

Fisch, S., Brinkhaus, B., & Teut, M. (2017). Hypnosis in patients with perceived stress: A systematic review. *BMC Complementary and Alternative Medicine, 17*(1), 323. https://doi.org/10.1186/s12906-017-1806-0

Fisch, S., Trivaković-Thiel, S., Roll, S., & et al. (2020). Group hypnosis for stress reduction and improved stress coping: A multicenter randomized controlled trial. *BMC Complementary Medicine and Therapies, 20*(1), 344. https://doi.org/10.1186/s12906-020-03129-6

Hasan, F. M., Zagarins, S. E., Pischke, K. M., Saiyed, S., Bettencourt, A. M., Beal, L., ... & McCleary, N. (2014). Hypnotherapy is more effective than nicotine replacement therapy for smoking cessation: Results of a randomized controlled trial. *Complementary Therapies in Medicine, 22*(1), 1-8. https://doi.org/10.1016/j.ctim.2013.12.012

National Center for Complementary and Integrative Health. (2024). *Press reset on stress*. National Institutes of Health. https://www.nccih.nih.gov/health/stress

Palsson, O. S., Turner, M. J., Johnson, D. A., Burnett, C. K., & Whitehead, W. E. (2002). Hypnosis treatment for severe irritable bowel syndrome: Investigation of mechanism and effects on symptoms. *Digestive Diseases and Sciences, 47*, 2605-2614. https://doi.org/10.1023/A:1020545017390

Chapter 14
Fears and Phobias

ALEX HOOD
CAMERON ALLDREDGE

Phobias involve an intense fear of a specific thing (like needles) or a certain situation (like flying in an airplane). About 12% of adults in the U.S. meet the criteria for the diagnosis of *specific phobia* at some point in their lives. When left untreated, phobias can be chronic and last many years, even decades. Hypnotherapy is an effective treatment option that helps empower individuals to face and overcome the things that cause immense fear.

Case Example – Camilla

Camilla was a 24-year-old married woman who sought hypnotherapy with me (CA) to help her with her severe phobia of spiders. Camilla had some bad experiences as a child being startled and frightened by large spiders. As an adult, she was constantly anxious that she might see a spider somewhere and was especially worried she would see one while showering in the bathroom. Her intense fear started to affect her day-to-day life because she stopped going outside out of fear that she might encounter a spider. She even began researching places in the country where she and her husband could move that reportedly have fewer spiders. Over time, she felt herself getting more anxious and simultaneously depressed.

What finally led her to seek treatment was an incident where she felt compelled to sell her couch because she had seen a spider about five feet away crawling toward her while she was sitting on it one day. She had heard about hypnotherapy and wanted to try it. She was highly motivated to overcome her fear and resume living her normal life. During the first session, it was noticeable that Camilla was so afraid of spiders that she could not even say the word "spider" out loud. Read on to discover how hypnotherapy helped Camilla and her spider phobia.

Phobias

Specific phobias are categorized based on what a person fears. One person may experience intense fear every time they get on or near an elevator—this would be a *situational* phobia. Another may experience overwhelming fear and run away when confronted with a snake—that's an *animal* phobia. Still another person might worry and feel panic when nature serves up a bad thunderstorm in their area—this is a *natural environment* phobia. Finally, someone might dread the doctor's office because they're deathly afraid of needles—this type is called a *blood-injection-injury* phobia. Patients with specific phobias can fear more than one thing, like flying on a plane *and* visiting the dentist. Across types, what specific phobias have in common is:

1. The fear and anxiety are excessive, which
2. cause changes to the way a person behaves, and
3. lead to significant distress and/or disruptions to their day-to-day functioning.

Usually, a person will change their behavior in a way that seems very logical—they'll *avoid* the thing that makes them scared. After all, not counting horror movies, excessive fear is no fun! However, it is this logical set of behaviors—called *avoidance behaviors*—that are chiefly responsible for keeping the phobia going. By steering clear of situations, objects, or environments the individual perceives as frightening, they are unintentionally training their brain to view these things as *even scarier*. This gives rise to a vicious cycle: Avoidance increases fear and anxiety, fear and anxiety increase avoidance, and on and on it goes.

Treatment of Specific Phobias

You may have been told as a kid to "face your fears!" *Exposure therapy*, the most common treatment for phobias, is based on this commonsense wisdom. It involves repeatedly putting a patient in front of the thing they fear, whether that be dogs, being at the top floor of a skyscraper, or going to a crowded shopping mall. The idea behind this method is not to torture the patient, but to show them that they can actually handle encounters with the things or situations they're afraid of. Exposure forms the backbone for most effective treatments for specific phobias. Treatments that use exposure often combine it with methods to promote learning to help people respond to things they fear in better ways.

Cognitive behavioral therapy (CBT) is another treatment that is geared toward making changes to how patients think about and respond to feared situations, objects, or environments. CBT therapists use a diverse set of techniques to challenge patients' predictions for and interpretations of experiences with the things they fear. Generally, therapies in the CBT family work well to lessen the symptoms of phobias.

Challenges to Treatment Success

There are many things that affect how a treatment will work for any given patient with a mental health concern. Examples include things like patient age, sex, severity of symptoms, expectations of therapy, prior treatment, and so on. Some of these things can be addressed in therapy and are therefore important for therapists to consider. For phobias in particular, there are two major parts of the therapy process that influence how effective the therapy is:

1. Early dropout from treatment, and
2. patients continuing to engage in (often subtle) avoidance behaviors.

Clearly, a person is going to see less benefit if they stop a treatment halfway through. It's not surprising that exposure-based therapies have high dropout rates as exposures are, by definition, distressing and unpleasant! Unfortunately, a patient stopping treatment early is yet another signal to their brain that the feared thing *really is dangerous* and needs to be avoided, making early dropout *doubly bad* for patients. Equally important are the *subtle avoidance behaviors* which are non-obvious things patients do to lessen their distress when facing situations, objects, or environments they're afraid of.

Hypnotherapy for Phobias

Hypnosis is a well-established treatment for specific phobias that compares well to other treatments. It's a good treatment all by itself but tends to be especially effective when combined with other techniques like exposure therapy or CBT. Many research studies have found that combining hypnosis with other treatments not only makes the treatments work *better*, but it makes them work *faster,* too. This means that therapists who use hypnosis when they treat phobias usually are able to do it in fewer sessions than those who don't. In addition, when hypnosis is used in the treatment of phobias, patients rate the treatment process as more pleasant overall, which is helpful when there's such a high risk of early dropout.

Hypnosis has been shown to be effective in lessening people's fear in many contexts. In particular, researchers have studied how hypnosis can help patients deal with intense fear in settings like hospitals, primary care clinics, and dental offices. Hypnosis has been successfully used to reduce fears related to medical procedures like surgeries, imaging procedures, needle sticks, and others. Among adults and children with *dental phobia*—that is, an intense fear of going to the dentist—hypnosis has a solid track record of reducing fears and making dental procedures tolerable.

How Does Hypnosis Help?

There are a few main ways that hypnosis can help in the treatment of phobias. First, it interrupts the fear response by giving patients more control over their thoughts and bodily sensations. Patients trained in self-hypnosis are able to remain relaxed in fear-provoking situations, making them less likely to engage in avoidance behaviors that—in the long run—make the fear worse. This more adaptive way of coping with stressful situations is a shortcut for patients to *learn new things* about what they fear, which is critical for successful treatment. Second, hypnosis can be used to improve patients' *self-concept*—it makes patients feel better about themselves, more capable, and more able to improve. Why might this be important for treatment? Well, remember what we said about *early treatment dropout* being a big problem for phobias? Therapy can ask a lot of a patient, and some patients—especially those who have had a specific phobia for a long time—feel disheartened and may doubt they'll ever get better. By working directly to build patients' belief that they're capable of improving, hypnosis lessens the likelihood of early dropout.

Hypnotherapy seems to provide the most help for phobias via exposure exercises that can be carried out while a person is in hypnosis. This is a favorable option for people because, in hypnosis, the exposure activities are experienced as if they are truly happening (e.g., it really feels like you're at the dentist's office) *and* it all happens within a safe and controlled environment. Clinicians can carefully tailor the exposure to start out at an easy level and gradually increase its intensity through hypnotic suggestions. Using hypnosis for exposure is usually a great preparatory step for folks as they move toward facing their phobia in real life.

Camilla's Hypnotherapy

Returning to the case of Camilla and her severe phobia of spiders, I (CA) used hypnosis for exposure exercises and for empowering Camilla to feel more confident about her ability to face spiders. For exposure exercises, the hypnosis made it possible to create specific situations for Camilla involving spiders that started off very easy (e.g., experiencing herself saying the word "spider") and progressed to circumstances that were more difficult and frightening (e.g., seeing a spider in the room or finding a spider crawling on her). In each instance, the hypnosis facilitated an experience that felt real to Camilla and gave her the opportunity to practice what she wanted her response to be.

Eventually, she began to feel more confident in her ability to handle seeing a spider. We met once a week for eight sessions and, by the end, the hypnotic suggestions sounded like this:

> *"Experience yourself doing something enjoyable inside your home... see, feel, and sense what it is like to spend your time doing something you like in the comfort of your home. In a few moments, you will look down and notice a spider crawling on the floor near you... You will notice that the sight of the spider is acceptable as you feel empowered to swiftly remove it from your home. See the spider, now, crawling on the floor... you can notice its size, color, and speed. Making these observations helps you to slow down your breathing and feel confident that you can handle this unwanted visitor... experience yourself calmly getting rid of the spider in whatever method seems most appropriate and safe. Notice how it feels to be calm and confident throughout the process... you're doing great. As you successfully excuse the spider from your home, you notice that you are able to quickly and easily return to the enjoyable activity you were engaged in previously... return to it with a sense of accomplishment and satisfaction... great job..."*

Chapter 14: Fears and Phobias

For our eighth and last session together, Camilla knew that I would be bringing a real spider to determine how successful the hypnotherapy had been for her. We discussed beforehand that we would try small experiments of looking at the spider in a closed container, holding the container with the spider, looking at the spider with container open, and perhaps letting the spider crawl freely on the floor of the therapy room. The morning of the session, I captured two decently sized spiders from my sprinkler box and brought them to the clinic in a plastic container.

As planned, the first task was having Camilla look at the spiders from a short distance while they were sealed in the container. She reported that this did not bother her at all, so we moved to the next task which involved Camilla holding the container. She did this with ease and eventually the two spiders were crawling around the therapy room, and she was completely unfazed. We celebrated for a moment as I gathered the spiders back into the container thinking our work was complete. Then, Camilla asked a question I never thought I'd hear her ask: "Can I try holding the spiders in my hand and let them go in the grass outside?"

I was shocked but gladly obliged. We walked to a grassy area right outside of the clinic and stood near the grass. I handed the container to Camilla who proceeded to reach her hand into it toward the spiders and hold it there until they climbed onto the back of her hand. They crawled around freely on her hands for a few moments, and she rotated her hands slowly to keep them in sight. Here was a person who, just two months prior, could not even say the word "spider." After a few moments of letting the spiders crawl around her hands, she knelt down and placed them gently into the grass.

Camilla was ecstatic and was able to continue living her life without the constant fear of seeing a spider. I heard from her months after we stopped meeting, and she informed me that she was still able to handle encounters with spiders with ease and that her overall wellbeing had improved dramatically.

Summary

Fears and phobias are very common mental health issues that often stick around as people avoid the things they're afraid of. Hypnosis has been shown to be an effective treatment for phobias that, when paired with other therapies, improves treatment outcomes, shortens treatment time, and makes treatment a more pleasant experience for patients. Hypnosis can be used to reduce avoidance, empower patients to help them stick with treatment, and facilitate impactful exposure exercises.

REFERENCES

Bandelow, B., Michaelis, S., & Wedekind, D. (2017). Treatment of anxiety disorders. *Dialogues in Clinical Neuroscience, 19*(2), 93–107. https://doi.org/10.31887/DCNS.2017.19.2/bbandelow

Depla, M. F., ten Have, M. L., van Balkom, A. J., & de Graaf, R. (2008). Specific fears and phobias in the general population: Results from the Netherlands Mental Health Survey and Incidence Study (NEMESIS). *Social Psychiatry and Psychiatric Epidemiology, 43*(3), 200–208. https://doi.org/10.1007/s00127-007-0291-z

Hammond D. C. (2010). Hypnosis in the treatment of anxiety- and stress-related disorders. *Expert Review of Neurotherapeutics, 10*(2), 263–273. https://doi.org/10.1586/ern.09.140

Kessler, R. C., Berglund, P., Chiu, W. T., Demler, O., Heeriga, S., Hiripi, E., Jin, R., Pennell, B. E., Walters, E. E., Zaslavsky, A., & Zheng, H. (2004). The US National Comorbidity Survey Replication (NCS-R): Design and field procedures. *International Journal of Methods in Psychiatric Research, 13*(2), 69–92. https://doi.org/10.1002/mpr.167

Spiegel D. (2013). Tranceformations: Hypnosis in brain and body. *Depression and Anxiety, 30*(4), 342–352. https://doi.org/10.1002/da.22046

Spiegel S. B. (2014). Current issues in the treatment of specific phobia: Recommendations for innovative applications of hypnosis. *The American Journal of Clinical Hypnosis, 56*(4), 389–404. https://doi.org/10.1080/00029157.2013.801009

Spiegel, S. (2017). Fear of flying. In G. R. Elkins (Ed.), *Handbook of medical and psychological hypnosis: Foundations, applications, and professional issues* (pp. 547-557). Springer Publishing Company.

Thomas P. McGuinness Ph.D. (1984) Hypnosis in the treatment of phobias: A review of the literature, *American Journal of Clinical Hypnosis*, *26*(4), 261-272. https://doi.org/10.1080/00029157.1984.10402574

Valentine, K. E., Milling, L. S., Clark, L. J., & Moriarty, C. L. (2019). The efficacy of hypnosis as a treatment for anxiety: A meta-analysis. *The International Journal of Clinical and Experimental Hypnosis*, *67*(3), 336–363. https://doi.org/10.1080/00207144.2019.1613863

Wetzer, G., Ten Have, M., de Graaf, R., Batelaan, N. M., & van Balkom, A. J. L. M. (2021). Specific phobia: Risk factor of other psychiatric disorders. *The Journal of Nervous and Mental Disease*, *209*(7), 484–490. https://doi.org/10.1097/NMD.0000000000001341

Wolf, T. G., Schläppi, S., Benz, C. I., & Campus, G. (2022). Efficacy of hypnosis on dental anxiety and phobia: A systematic review and meta-analysis. *Brain Sciences*, *12*(5), 521. https://doi.org/10.3390/brainsci12050521

Chapter 15
Anxiety and Depression

Katherine Scheffrahn
Gary Elkins

Anxiety and depression are the most common emotional problems for which people seek counseling or other treatment. In fact, at some time in their lives, most people experience some concerns about anxiety, depression, or both. Anxiety can range from mild to very severe and the same is true for depression. However, anxiety and depression are treatable, and there is support through hypnotherapy interventions as well as cognitive-behavioral therapy (CBT) and medications. In this chapter, we review facts and information about anxiety and depression and provide an understanding on how hypnotherapy can be of significant help.

Anxiety

First, let's talk about anxiety. When confronted with some danger, anxiety serves a purpose in our lives by making us aware of and ready to react to potential danger. This is sometimes called the "fight or flight response." However, anxiety can persist even when the danger has passed or if we begin to worry and ruminate about possible threatening future events. Anxiety disorders occur when the anxiety does not go away and begins to interfere with daily life. In the United States, it is estimated that generalized anxiety disorder (GAD) affects 6.8 million adults, but less than half of these seek treatment. For social anxiety, the numbers are even larger, with over 15 million U.S. adults suffering from social anxiety disorder. Further, anxiety is closely associated with stress, which is so pervasive that the American Psychological Association has called stress in the U.S. "a national mental health crisis." It is imperative that people recognize the stress and anxiety in their lives and learn how to deal with it effectively. There are several types of anxiety disorders: generalized anxiety disorder, panic disorder, social anxiety disorder, and phobia-related disorders. Below are brief descriptions of each.

Generalized anxiety disorder (GAD) is when a person experiences persistent anxiety or dread. Symptoms could include:

- Difficulty controlling symptoms of worry
- Restlessness
- Fatigue
- Irritability
- Difficulty concentrating
- Headaches, muscle aches, or unexplained pains
- Sleep issues, such as difficulty falling asleep or staying asleep

Social anxiety disorder is when a person experiences great anxiety specifically in social situations. People may fear being watched or judged by other people while in those situations; many individuals with social anxiety disorder report avoiding social situations as much as possible due to their anxiety. Phobia-related disorders are the intense fear of specific objects or situations. Often, the person's fear is out of proportion with what the situation calls for or is irrational in some way. Panic disorder is when a person is experiencing frequent panic attacks, even when there is no cause for panic. Panic attacks are sudden feelings of intense fear, often accompanied by a pounding heart, sweating, chest pain, and feelings of being out of control.

It is also true that anxiety and depression are often experienced at the same time. In fact, chronic anxiety related to worry, loss, or fear can lead to feelings of hopelessness and depression. Anxiety and depression can be co-morbid and so intertwined that it can be hard to fully distinguish one from the other. However, distinct from anxiety, depression involves more feelings of sadness, hopelessness, and negative perceptions about the past, present, and/or the future. We now will look more closely at depression.

Depression

Over 264 million people worldwide suffer from depression. In the United States alone, over 18 million adults have experienced one or more major depressive episodes. In fact, depression can be so severe that it is now the leading cause of disability in adolescents and middle-aged adults. Depression can arise out of many difficult situations—going through a divorce, loss of a loved one, loss of job or career, or ruminating about stresses and difficulties. Depression occurs in both men and women, but at a higher rate in women. Perhaps this is due to the multiple stresses and expectations that society places on women to a greater degree than on men regarding balancing work, family, and relationships. When depressed, men are more likely than women to experience feelings of irritability, anger, or physical symptoms such as feeling tired and withdrawing from others; men are also more likely to turn to alcohol or substance use in an attempt to avoid the pain of depression. It is important to be on the look-out for depression in yourself and others as it can manifest in different ways. Though depression is often portrayed somewhat simplistically as a person just feeling sadness, depression includes many other symptoms. If you experience some of the following symptoms nearly every day for at least two weeks, you may be experiencing depression. Symptoms may include:

- Persistent sadness, anxiety, or empty mood
- Feeling of hopelessness or pessimism
- Feelings of irritability, frustration, or restlessness
- Loss of interest or pleasure in hobbies and activities
- Fatigue, lack of energy, or feeling slowed down
- Difficulty concentrating, remembering, or making decisions
- Difficulty sleeping, waking too early in the morning, or oversleeping
- Changes in appetite or unplanned weight changes
- Physical aches or pains, headaches, cramps, or digestive problems without a clear physical cause that do not go away with treatment
- Increased engagement in high-risk activities
- Increased anger or irritability
- Feeling restless or on edge
- Becoming withdrawn, negative, or detached
- Greater impulsivity
- Increased use of alcohol or drugs
- Isolating from family and friends
- Problems with sexual desire and performance
- Inability to meet the responsibilities of work and family or ignoring other important roles
- Thoughts of death or suicide attempts

If you are struggling with depression, receiving help and treatment may be right for you. However, if you are experiencing thoughts of death or suicide, you should immediately contact a healthcare professional or go to a hospital emergency room for services.

How can Hypnotherapy Help to Cope with and Reduce Anxiety and Depression?

When undergoing hypnotherapy for anxiety or depression, a clinical therapist or counselor will collaborate with you to discuss your symptoms and treatment priorities. After that, the hypnotherapist will lead you in a hypnotic induction, where you will be directed to focus your attention and relax. While undergoing hypnosis, the hypnotherapist will lead you through techniques shown by research to treat anxiety and depression, such as ego-strengthening, expansion of awareness, and positive mood induction. Ego-strengthening suggestions are meant to help grow your self-esteem and self-efficacy, which is your confidence in being able to cope successfully with challenging situations. Expansion of awareness involves suggestions crafted to bring underlying emotions into conscious awareness, bringing awareness to certain feelings, increasing motivation, and intensifying positive moods. Positive mood induction is where hypnosis helps you form positive associations in the brain to combat the negative thought spirals associated with anxiety and depression. These suggestions will help improve your mood over time and decrease your experience of this negative rumination.

You may also learn how to use self-hypnosis. Self-hypnosis is a helpful tool that will allow you to use hypnosis on your own at home. This would involve the hypnotherapist teaching you the basic skills of hypnosis, including relaxation, imagery, and suggestion, and giving you ways to practice these on your own. Self-hypnosis is a beneficial skill because it gives you the ability to build coping skills and prepare for stressful events.

Digital Hypnotherapy for Mental Health

Claria is a digital hypnotherapy app created by Mindset Health to help people manage their mental health. Dr. Michael Yapko, a clinical hypnosis researcher and psychologist, helped develop the app, and its five-week hypnotherapy program is based directly on the research on how hypnotherapy can help with anxiety and depression. The Claria app works to help you develop 12 essential skills to empower yourself to deal with anxiety and depression. The 12 essential skills include:

- Setting positive expectations
- Developing patience
- Learning to tolerate uncertainty
- Taking positive actions and behaviors
- Redefining your self-image
- Making good decisions
- Countering helplessness
- Thinking more clearly
- Thinking ahead
- Being curious and less fearful
- Improving sleep
- Building strong relationships

What the Science Says about Hypnotherapy for Anxiety and Depression

A 2019 meta-analysis—which is an article where several studies are evaluated at once to understand if a treatment is effective—examined studies where hypnosis was used to treat anxiety. In these studies, hypnosis for anxiety was compared to a control condition where people were either receiving no treatment or a different treatment for anxiety. The results showed that hypnosis is a highly effective treatment for anxiety symptoms. The average participant who received hypnosis showed more symptom improvement than 79% of the control participants. This review also confirmed that hypnosis is just as effective as CBT in treating anxiety symptoms. A different meta-analysis examined hypnosis as a treatment for depression symptoms. This review evaluated

13 trials of hypnosis compared to a control condition. They found that, on average, participants receiving hypnosis showed more symptom improvement than 76% of the control participants. They also showed that the benefits persisted after the end of the study; when looking at a trial with a nine-month follow-up with the participants, those treated with hypnosis still showed greater symptom improvement on average than the control group. These results also demonstrated that hypnosis for depression is comparable to other common psychological interventions such as CBT. The authors of the meta-analysis claim that this suggests hypnosis is a very effective way of alleviating symptoms of depression.

One study randomly assigned 152 participants to receive either CBT or hypnotherapy for their depression. This study found that 45% of participants treated with hypnotherapy saw a reduction of at least 50% in their symptoms, while only 39% of the CBT participants saw a reduction of at least 50%. When the researchers followed up with the participants after 12 months, 67.6% of the patients who received hypnotherapy were still in full remission of their depression, which is far higher than the 22% to 40% reduction rate of remitted patients treated with antidepressants. Several studies have shown hypnotherapy apps to be helpful with medical and psychological disorders, so Claria also may provide an easily accessible hypnotherapy option. Research is ongoing!

Case Example – Ella

Ella is a 33-year-old woman who, throughout her life, would have described herself as a happy and content individual. After graduating college, Ella married her college sweetheart, and the couple has a tight-knit community of family and friends. Ella loves to play board games and go on long-distance runs with her two big dogs that the couple adopted. Six months ago, Ella was promoted to a new role at the publishing firm where she works. Ella worked hard to earn the promotion, but the new role came with heightened pressure and scrutiny from her higher-ups.

After the promotion, Ella began to have trouble concentrating on her work, finding herself being overrun with anxiety, worry, and fatigue. As her new role intensified, Ella began to feel a constant sense of dread even when she was trying to spend time with her husband or friends. Though usually a heavy sleeper, Ella began to struggle shutting her thoughts off to go to sleep at night. Ella became aware that something was wrong, and she decided to seek help from her physician.

Ella and her physician recognized that she was struggling with anxiety and depression. Ella told her therapist that she did not want to use antidepressants or anxiolytic medication because she was aware that there were many side effects associated with pharmaceuticals. Her physician agreed and suggested Ella try hypnotherapy, as it was a psychotherapeutic treatment that did not have risk of negative side effects.

At Ella's first hypnotherapy appointment, her hypnotherapist asked questions about her symptoms and asked about the new job position that had instigated the change in her mental health. Ella visited her hypnotherapist once per week, and after five weeks, she noticed her anxiety had lessened, allowing her to sleep much better. During one of her appointments, her hypnotherapist began teaching her how to engage in self-hypnosis on her own to provide support in addition to her appointments. Ella found the self-hypnosis very helpful; after stressful work meetings, when she felt her thoughts begin to spiral, she could practice self-hypnosis to help return herself to a more regulated state. Ella's therapist suggested that she might also use the Claria app for daily hypnosis sessions. She found this to be a helpful and easy way to access hypnotherapy sessions focused on specific skills. Ella's anxiety and depression symptoms decreased, but she wanted to continue using self-hypnosis at home with the Claria app to support her mental health. Now, she feels much better and continues to use self-hypnosis to help her manage the stresses of life.

Summary

Research has shown that hypnotherapy is very beneficial for both anxiety and depression. Many people want to feel more empowered to better manage their stress, anxiety, and feelings of depression. Hypnotherapy provides a pleasant, beneficial treatment that can be used alone or in combination with counseling or psychotherapy. If you find yourself experiencing symptoms of anxiety or depression, consider seeking out a hypnotherapist. If finding a hypnotherapist is challenging, the Claria smartphone app provides an easily accessible way to use hypnosis to support mental health.

REFERENCES

Alladin, A. (2009). Evidence-based cognitive hypnotherapy for depression. *Contemporary Hypnosis*, *26*(4), 245–262. https://doi.org/10.1002/ch.391

Alladin, A. (2010). Evidence-based hypnotherapy for depression. *International Journal of Clinical and Experimental Hypnosis*, *58*(2), 165–185. https://doi.org/10.1080/00207140903523194

American Psychological Association (2020). Stress in America: A national health crisis. https://www.apa.org/news/press/releases/stress/2020/sia-mental-health-crisis.pdf

Burkhard, P. (2017) Anxieties in adults. In G. R. Elkins (Ed.), *Handbook of medical and psychological hypnosis: Foundations, applications, and professional issues* (pp. 469–476). Springer Publishing Company.

Fuhr, K., Meisner, C., & Batra, A. (2023). Long-term outcomes of depression treatment with hypnotherapy or cognitive behavioral therapy. *Journal of Nervous and Mental Disease*, *211*(7), 519. https://doi.org/10.1097/NMD.0000000000001647

Fuhr, K., Meisner, C., Broch, A., Cyrny, B., Hinkel, J., Jaberg, J., Petrasch, M., Schweizer, C., Stiegler, A., Zeep, C., & Batra, A. (2021). Efficacy of hypnotherapy compared to cognitive behavioral therapy for mild to moderate depression—Results of a randomized controlled rater-blind clinical trial. *Journal of Affective Disorders*, *286*, 166–173. https://doi.org/10.1016/j.jad.2021.02.069

Golden, W. L. (2012). Cognitive hypnotherapy for anxiety disorders. *American Journal of Clinical Hypnosis*, *54*(4), 263–274. https://doi.org/10.1080/00029157.2011.650333

Kaufman, J., & Charney, D. (2000). Comorbidity of mood and anxiety disorders. *Depression and Anxiety*, *12*(S1), 69–76. https://doi.org/10.1002/1520-6394(2000)12:1+<69::AID-DA9>3.0.CO;2-K

Mendlewicz, J. (2008). Towards achieving remission in the treatment of depression. *Dialogues in Clinical Neuroscience*, *10*(4), 371–375. https://doi.org/10.31887/DCNS.2008.10.4/jmendlewicz

Milling, L. S., Valentine, K. E., McCarley, H. S., & LoStimolo, L. M. (2019). A meta-analysis of hypnotic interventions for depression symptoms: High hopes for hypnosis? *American Journal of Clinical Hypnosis*, *61*(3), 227–243. https://doi.org/10.1080/00029157.2018.1489777

National Institute of Mental Health. (March, 2024). *Depression*. https://www.nimh.nih.gov/health/topics/depression

National Institute of Mental Health. (March, 2024). *Major Depression*. https://www.nimh.nih.gov/health/statistics/major-depression

National Institute of Mental Health. (June, 2024). *Statistics—Any Anxiety Disorder*. https://www.nimh.nih.gov/health/statistics/any-anxiety-disorder

Torem, M. (2017) Depression. In G. R. Elkins (Ed.), *Handbook of Medical and Psychological Hypnosis: Foundations, Applications, and Professional Issues* (pp. 505–521). Springer Publishing Company.

Valentine, K. E., Milling, L. S., Clark, L. J., & Moriarty, C. L. (2019). The efficacy of hypnosis as a treatment for anxiety: A meta-analysis. *International Journal of Clinical and Experimental Hypnosis*, *67*(3), 336–363. https://doi.org/10.1080/00207144.2019.1613863

Chapter 16
Chronic Pain

KATHERINE SCHEFFRAHN
CAMERON ALLDREDGE

Chronic pain is among the most common and challenging health issues in the United States. Approximately 20.5% of adults in the U.S.—around 50.2 million people—report experiencing pain on most days. This means that one in every five Americans is experiencing some form of chronic pain. Of greater concern is that 6.9% of U.S. adults—approximately 17.1 million people—experience pain that is severe enough to significantly restrict their daily activities. Chronic pain affects some groups more than others; women, older adults, adults with lower socioeconomic status, and residents of rural areas have a higher prevalence of chronic pain than the overall population.

The Impact and Treatment of Chronic Pain

Chronic pain can be incredibly impactful in all areas of life. For individuals with persistent pain, it can negatively affect work, relationships, social life, sleep, and overall mental health. People with chronic pain report missing 3.5 times as many days of work compared to people without chronic pain. Relationally, individuals with chronic pain can find it challenging to be active and spend time with friends or family. Additionally, most people with chronic pain experience sleep disturbances due to pain or discomfort while they are trying to sleep. Symptoms of anxiety and depression have also been linked to chronic pain and individuals with long-lasting chronic pain are at increased risk for suicide.

There are many different modalities for treating chronic pain, and people often use multiple methods simultaneously to provide relief. Commonly used treatments include analgesic and narcotic medications. While these medications can help reduce pain, they can also lead to dependency and addiction. Further, pain medications are not effective for all persons. For these reasons, many people seek alternatives or complementary ways to manage chronic pain. This can include physical therapy, massage therapy, meditation, acupuncture, and of course, hypnotherapy. Hypnotherapy can be a very beneficial approach, and there are decades of research demonstrating how well it can work for individuals experiencing chronic pain.

Can Hypnotherapy Help Manage Chronic Pain?

Hypnotherapy is a good treatment option for several reasons. First, hypnotherapy does not burden a chronic pain patient with any additional side effects—something that cannot be said about many pharmaceutical solutions. Additionally, hypnosis has no addictive potential, which remains a problem with many stronger pain medications that have contributed to the current opioid crisis. Hypnotherapy also involves the patient learning the skills to utilize self-hypnosis for their pain, which allows a greater amount of self-sufficiency for individuals experiencing chronic pain.

Hypnotherapy sessions typically utilize suggestions for pain relief; for example, a hypnotherapist might suggest feeling the pain "dimming" or "putting the pain in a box." Another popular approach is called *glove anesthesia* which involves the experience of numbness that starts in the hand and spreads to other areas of the body needing pain relief. Other hypnotic strategies for pain reduction may include changing the painful sensations to something else, such as pressure or coolness, increasing feelings of comfort, and increasing one's ability to ignore pain. Clinicians also often give suggestions to help individuals increase their ability to engage in activities that their pain might otherwise limit. Moreover, hypnotherapy may include suggestions that are designed to alter negative perceptions about the pain and increase one's ability to emotionally cope with the experience of chronic pain.

Typically, hypnotic suggestions are delivered in a way that extends their impact to continue taking effect even when the hypnosis has ended. Although it is common not to see drastic changes after the first session, most people report that they begin to notice decreases in chronic pain after just a few sessions. The ability to learn how to use the skill of self-hypnosis also helps relieve chronic pain long-term. Self-hypnosis can be learned throughout treatment, which may include the use of audio recordings for at-home practice. Chronic pain is often a persistent challenge in the lives of patients, and self-hypnosis is a tool that can allow patients to take back some agency and control in their treatment.

Digital Hypnotherapy for Chronic Pain

The Relio app is a digital hypnotherapy app that was designed with experts based on scientific research to facilitate self-administered hypnotherapy for chronic pain management. Though Relio is targeted specifically for chronic back pain, it may also assist with other chronic pain conditions by helping to calm an overreactive pain system in the body. The audio recordings provided in the app are an easily accessible way to try hypnotherapy. For someone curious about trying hypnosis for chronic pain, this could be a great place to start.

What the Science Says About Hypnosis for Pain Management

Hypnosis has been used as a treatment for pain since the 1840s, when it was first systematically used as an analgesic. Today, the treatment of pain is one of the most well-researched areas of hypnosis and remains one of its best use cases. It has been examined in over 66 studies involving more than 3,000 participants. A recently published review article combined the findings from five meta-analyses on hypnosis for pain and found that hypnosis was able to effectively reduce participants' pain intensity. One of the meta-analyses included in this synthesis was published in 2021 and looked at 45 different trials of hypnosis for pain; the meta-analysis concluded that "hypnosis is a very efficacious intervention for alleviating clinical pain." These researchers found evidence to suggest that the effects of hypnosis are long-lasting and that individuals of higher hypnotizability will likely experience more benefit with hypnosis compared to other psychological approaches.

Let's look more closely at the kinds of chronic pain found to be treatable by hypnotherapy. A 2022 systematic review and meta-analysis, which summarized nine studies examining various types of pain, found that hypnosis helped to relieve pain-related conditions such as back pain, osteoarthritis, multiple sclerosis, spinal cord injury pain, brachial neuralgia, and hemarthrosis (irreversible muscle or joint damage). This research also indicated that patients who received 8 or more hypnosis sessions experienced a more significant and lasting reduction in their pain. Another systematic review looked at 12 clinical trials of hypnosis for chronic pain and found that hypnosis reduced pain for conditions such as osteoarthritis pain, spinal cord injury chronic pain, multiple sclerosis, and non-cardiac chest pain. Research has also shown that hypnosis can help reduce pain stemming from fibromyalgia, migraines, arthritis, neuropathic pain, endometriosis, and chronic pain in cancer survivors.

Case Example – Carl

An example of hypnotherapy for chronic pain management is illustrated in the case of Carl (seen by one of the authors, GE). Carl was in his mid-40s when he began to experience discomfort in his lower back. He

Chapter 16: Chronic Pain

especially noticed it after doing yard work, mowing, or lifting. He was generally able to manage the pain with over-the-counter medications and rest. However, at age 50 he was involved in a car accident in which his car was rear-ended by another driver. He went to the emergency room after the accident and underwent x-rays and examination and was sent home with a prescription for hydrocodone. He found the medication eased the pain, only for the pain to return as the effect wore off within a few hours. Carl was able to return to work but found the pain getting worse. He was taking pain medications every day to try to cope with the lower back pain. His physician became concerned that Carl was becoming dependent on the hydrocodone, but there were few alternatives. He was seen for a surgery consult and it was noted that he had a bulging disc in his lower back. He underwent surgery and initially had a positive result, only for the pain to return. Carl then had a discussion with his physician about how to cope with the pain and alternatives. His physician suggested he try hypnotherapy, as research has shown it to be of benefit for chronic pain in some patients.

The next week, Carl saw a health psychologist who specialized in chronic pain management and clinical hypnosis. In the first session, a hypnotic induction was completed with suggestions for deep relaxation, analgesia (numbness) in his lower back, and visualizing "turning the pain dial down." At the end of the session, he felt his pain was reduced and was encouraged. Carl had 12 hypnotherapy sessions that were focused on relaxation, pain reduction, improving sleep, and learning self-hypnosis. He also began using the Relio app for self-hypnosis and hypnosis audio recordings for home practice. Carl found this to be especially helpful and he was able to gradually reduce his use of pain medications to a minimal level. Carl and his physician were pleased with his progress. Carl found that he could use self-hypnosis to better manage his pain and do the things he wanted to do. However, he was cautioned to "not overdo it," and he hired someone to do his mowing and yard work. With these changes—daily practice of self-hypnosis, taking better care of himself and accepting his physical limitations, and reducing his dependency on pain medications—Carl was able to resume a normal life. His sleep was better, he felt more relaxed, and pain was under control.

Summary

Chronic pain impacts millions of people and tends to interfere with work and social life in a way that reduces overall wellbeing. Treatment for chronic pain is important to help combat some of the issues that chronic pain patients experience, but traditional pharmaceutical approaches may not be for everyone. Treating pain is one of the most researched uses for clinical hypnosis. Past studies have demonstrated that hypnotherapy can safely and effectively treat a wide variety of pain-related concerns with lasting effects.

REFERENCES

Adachi, T., Fujino, H., Nakae, A., Mashimo, T., & Sasaki1, J. (2014). A meta-analysis of hypnosis for chronic pain problems: A comparison between hypnosis, standard care, and other psychological interventions. *International Journal of Clinical and Experimental Hypnosis, 62*(1), 1–28. https://doi.org/10.1080/00207144.2013.841471

Aravena, V., García, F. E., Téllez, A., & Arias, P. R. (2020). Hypnotic intervention in people with fibromyalgia: A randomized controlled trial. *American Journal of Clinical Hypnosis, 63*(1), 49–61. https://doi.org/10.1080/00029157.2020.1742088

Cleveland Clinic. (2021). *What is it, causes, symptoms & treatment.* Chronic Pain. https://my.clevelandclinic.org/health/diseases/4798-chronic-pain

Dahlhamer, J. (2018). Prevalence of chronic pain and high-impact chronic pain among adults—United States, 2016. *Morbidity and Mortality Weekly Report,* 67. https://doi.org/10.15585/mmwr.mm6736a2

Dowell, D. (2022). CDC clinical practice guideline for prescribing opioids for pain—United States, 2022. *Morbidity and Mortality Weekly Report, 71.* https://doi.org/10.15585/mmwr.rr7103a1

Eaton, L. H., Jang, M. K., Jensen, M. P., Pike, K. C., Heitkemper, M. M., & Doorenbos, A. Z. (2022). Hypnosis and relaxation interventions for chronic pain management in cancer survivors: A randomized controlled trial. *Supportive Care in Cancer, 31*(1), 50. https://doi.org/10.1007/s00520-022-07498-1

Flynn, N. (2018). Systematic review of the effectiveness of hypnosis for the management of headache. *International Journal of Clinical and Experimental Hypnosis, 66*(4), 343–352. https://doi.org/10.1080/00207144.2018.1494432

Hadi, M. A., McHugh, G. A., & Closs, S. J. (2019). Impact of chronic pain on patients' quality of life: A comparative mixed-methods study. *Patient Experience, 6*(2), 133–141. https://doi.org/10.1177/2374373518786013

Horton-Hausknecht, J. R., Mitzdorf, U., & Melchart, D. (2000). The effect of hypnosis therapy on the symptoms and disease activity in Rheumatoid Arthritis. *Psychology & Health, 14*(6), 1089–1104. https://doi.org/10.1080/08870440008407369

Jensen, M. (2017). Pain management—chronic pain. In G. R. Elkins (Ed.), *Handbook of Medical and Psychological Hypnosis: Foundations, Applications, and Professional Issues* (pp. 341-360). Springer Publishing Company.

Johns Hopkins Medicine. (2024, May 24). *Chronic pain*. Health. https://www.hopkinsmedicine.org/health/conditions-and-diseases/chronic-pain

Langlois, P., Perrochon, A., David, R., Rainville, P., Wood, C., Vanhaudenhuyse, A., Pageaux, B., Ounajim, A., Lavallière, M., Debarnot, U., Luque-Moreno, C., Roulaud, M., Simoneau, M., Goudman, L., Moens, M., Rigoard, P., & Billot, M. (2022). Hypnosis to manage musculoskeletal and neuropathic chronic pain: A systematic review and meta-analysis. *Neuroscience & Biobehavioral Reviews, 135*, 104591. https://doi.org/10.1016/j.neubiorev.2022.104591

Lee, J. S., & Pyun, Y. D. (2012). Use of hypnosis in the treatment of pain. *Korean Journal of Pain, 25*(2), 75–80. https://doi.org/10.3344/kjp.2012.25.2.75

McCracken, L. M., & Iverson, G. L. (2002). Disrupted sleep patterns and daily functioning in patients with chronic pain. *Pain Research and Management, 7*(2), 579425. https://doi.org/10.1155/2002/579425

McKittrick, M. L., Connors, E. L., & McKernan, L. C. (2022). Hypnosis for chronic neuropathic pain: A scoping review. *Pain Medicine, 23*(5), 1015–1026. https://doi.org/10.1093/pm/pnab320

Rikard, S. M. (2023). Chronic pain among adults—United States, 2019–2021. *Morbidity and Mortality Weekly Report, 72*. https://doi.org/10.15585/mmwr.mm7215a1

Rosendahl, J., Alldredge, C. T., & Haddenhorst, A. (2024). Meta-analytic evidence on the efficacy of hypnosis for mental and somatic health issues: A 20-year perspective. *Frontiers in Psychology, 14*, 1330238. https://doi.org/10.3389/fpsyg.2023.1330238

Shahriyaripoor, R., Shahhosseini, Z., Pourasghar, M., Hoseinnezhad, Z., Shahriyaripoor, R., & Ganji, J. (2023). The effect of hypnotherapy on the pain intensity of endometriosis patients treated with dienogest: A pilot double-blind randomized clinical trial. *Journal of Nursing and Midwifery Sciences, 10*(4), Article 4. https://doi.org/10.5812/jnms-137116

Vickers, A. J., Vertosick, E. A., Lewith, G., MacPherson, H., Foster, N. E., Sherman, K. J., Irnich, D., Witt, C. M., Linde, K., & Acupuncture Trialists' Collaboration. (2018). Acupuncture for chronic pain: Update of an individual patient data meta-analysis. *Pain, 19*(5), 455–474. https://doi.org/10.1016/j.jpain.2017.11.005

Yong, R. J., Mullins, P. M., & Bhattacharyya, N. (2022). Prevalence of chronic pain among adults in the United States. *Pain, 163*(2), e328–e332. https://doi.org/10.1097/j.pain.0000000000002291

Chapter 17
Mindfulness and Hypnosis

Gary Elkins
Victor Julian Padilla

From meditation apps to guided meditations on YouTube, mindfulness has seen a surge in popularity in mental health care over the past two decades. Mindfulness has been defined as the practice of observing your thoughts, emotions, and actions in a nonjudgmental way and with an open attitude of acceptance. It involves learning to observe and accept thoughts and feelings which results in decreased stress and greater mindfulness in everyday activities. By practicing mindfulness regularly, you may begin to notice a variety of positive changes to your health. It is a habit that you can incorporate into your daily routine with little risk and without needing any specialized equipment or extensive training. Regular mindfulness practice has been shown to be beneficial for improving stress, anxiety, depression, pain management, and general satisfaction with life among other things. These changes have been noted in novice meditators starting out their journey, and they continue to improve as they become accustomed to focusing their attention and meditating more often and for longer.

Mindfulness meditation is what usually is identified when someone mentions practicing mindfulness. However, you may be able to boost your mindfulness practice with hypnotherapy. Mindful hypnotherapy involves learning how to use self-hypnosis toward mindfulness goals. Regular practice of mindful self-hypnosis can not only enhance increased mindfulness, but it can also reduce stress and cause positive change when encountering difficulties in work, home, or social life. More about mindful hypnotherapy follows below!

Mindful Hypnotherapy: The Intersection of Mindfulness and Hypnosis

Given their shared use of focused attention, researchers and clinicians have collaborated to combine elements of different mindfulness techniques with hypnotic suggestions to develop an innovative new type of intervention called mindful hypnotherapy. Why add hypnotic suggestions to enhance mindfulness practice? Meditation by itself can be very difficult for novices or those going through intense emotional experiences. Adding guided hypnotic suggestions to your mindfulness practice may help ease you into a deeper level of meditation faster and with less resistance. This can make it easier to focus your attention, nonjudgmentally observe your own thoughts and feelings, and achieve deeper relaxation. Learning mindful self-hypnosis may also have the added benefit of being very goal directed by nature. If you are looking to change a behavior or mindset moving forward, you can incorporate mindful self-hypnosis, customized to your specific goals, into your mindful hypnotherapy sessions to help guide you toward success.

Case Example – Esteban

Esteban is a 20-year-old college student who frequently has trouble managing his stress levels during his day-to-day life. He was grateful to have been accepted to his top choice for university, but the constant influx of new projects and deadlines quickly became overwhelming. By the end of his sophomore year Esteban felt guilty if he did not spend most of his day studying at the library. He made less and less time for himself to socialize, eat, and sleep out of fear of getting behind in his work. His attempts at forcing himself to sit down and relax usually left him feeling nauseous as thoughts of failure flooded his mind. It was easier for him to spend his free time preparing for future exams and assignments even if they were more than a month away. Over the past three months, Esteban has tried a variety of different medications and exercises to help him reduce his stress, but he has yet to find a combination that sits right with him. Meditation was especially difficult for Esteban since he had trouble sitting with his stress for long periods of time. His therapist recommended that he try mindful hypnotherapy to help him better manage his stress.

After hearing about mindful hypnotherapy and its potential benefits from his therapist, Esteban decided to enroll in a clinical trial at the Baylor Mind-Body Medicine Research Laboratory on a brief mindful hypnotherapy intervention for stress reduction. Esteban was surprised by how seamless and pleasant the hypnotic induction was. His interventionist asked him to focus on a spot on the ceiling then eased him into a state of deep relaxation by guiding him through a mindful breathing exercise. The rest of the session passed quickly as they went over ways to disengage from stressful thoughts and emotions.

One month after his mindful hypnotherapy session, Esteban was happy to report that it had become much easier for him to manage his stress. He confessed that he would occasionally still get knots in stomach whenever he received a lot of homework at once, but he felt much more confident in his ability to let these feelings pass. He no longer felt guilty if he did not dedicate his entire day to studying. Slowly, he was getting back into the rhythm of making time to cook, exercise, and spend time having fun with his peers without having to worry about getting behind academically.

What is the Science Behind Mindful Hypnotherapy?

Mindful hypnotherapy is a relatively new and innovative approach to enhancing mindfulness practice. A recent study examined the effect of the practice of mindful self-hypnosis on reducing stress and increasing mindfulness in college students. Fifty-five college students were randomly assigned to be in either a mindful hypnotherapy condition or a waitlist control condition. The mindful hypnotherapy condition consisted of eight weekly hour-long sessions which covered topics such as bodily awareness, relaxation, and self-compassion. Participants in this group received audio recordings with instructions for a self-administered mindful hypnosis practice at the end of each session to practice with at home. Compared to participants assigned to the waitlist condition, participants in the mindful hypnotherapy intervention reported significantly lower perceived stress, lower psychological distress, and higher mindfulness scores at their follow-up session than they had during their baseline session. Another recent study found that mindful hypnotherapy is useful in reducing stress and improving mindfulness even when the participants received just a single session. The positive effects that mindful hypnotherapy has on improving pain management, emotion regulation, and other health outcomes continue to be the topic of ongoing research.

Personal Experience with Mindful Hypnotherapy

As a graduate student, I (VJP) can have a hard time getting out of my own head. Assisting with clinical trials, grading my students' papers, conducting my own research, and preparing manuscripts for publication is challenging to manage. Even as someone who has been meditating for years, it can be difficult for me to sit down and focus on my breathing when thoughts on upcoming tasks are always scratching at the side of my mind. What has helped me the most in recent years has been using a short self-hypnotic induction at the start of my mindful self-hypnosis sessions to help me release stress. I have used this technique so often that I became curious about the mechanisms behind mindful hypnotherapy and ended up selecting mindful hypnotherapy as the topic for my dissertation. Below, I have included a brief mindful hypnosis exercise to try out on your own at home or whenever you are feeling overwhelmed by stress.

Practice: Mindful self-hypnosis for relaxation and stress reduction

1. Take a moment to pick a spot around you. It can be a plant, a smudge on the ceiling, or a piece of furniture. Anything will do. Allow yourself to focus your attention entirely on that object and let everything else just fade away into your periphery.

2. Take a deep long breath and let your eyelids close as you exhale.

3. Notice the sensation of air leaving your lungs.

4. Breathe in again to the count of four, hold your breath for a moment, and breath out to the count of four

5. With one part of your mind, you can continue to breathe in and out in this steady rhythm while with another part of your mind you can mindfully observe the sensations in your body.

6. With every breath you take, fill your lungs with relaxation. Let it spread throughout your body from your lungs out to your shoulder... your arms... and your hands and fingers...all parts of upper body... then moving down chest to your lower body... relaxing all of the muscles down yours legs... your feet and toes... Allow all of the tension in your body to dissipate with every inhalation, and let go of any stress and tension out though your nose and mouth as you exhale... If you notice that there is a part of you that feels especially

tense or tight, feel free to take as much time as you need to breathe soothing relaxation into that spot... and breath out any of the tension that was stored there... You can spend as much or as little time observing any part of your body.

7. If any distressing thoughts...memories... or feelings arise, allow them to drift with your breath... through your lungs... and out of your body... just observe them as they pass on by. You can do this effortlessly without judgement. Accept them... let them be... and soon they will pass each and every time that they arise... Gently guide your focus back to your breathing.

8. When you are ready, slowly bring yourself back to conscious alertness and open your eyes...take your time... there is no need to rush... You will soon feel fully alert... and you can take all of the relaxation and mindfulness that you have cultivated in your body through this exercise with you as you do so... For the rest of today, you will be able to be more at ease and more confident in your ability to manage your stress. If you need to take a moment to shake your arms and legs awake, feel free to do so before continuing with the rest of your day.

Summary

Mindful hypnotherapy effectively combines techniques from standard mindfulness practice with hypnotic suggestions to provide a safe and easy way to help improve your mental health. Research on the effects of mindful hypnotherapy is in its early stages, but the findings from the studies published thus far are very promising. I hope that the information that we have provided you in this chapter will serve you well moving forward.

REFERENCES

Elkins, G. R., & Olendzki, N. (2019). *Mindful hypnotherapy: The basics for clinical practice* (pp. xvi, 278). Springer Publishing Company.

Khazraee, H., Bakhtiari, M., Kianimoghadam, A. S., & Hajmanouchehri, R. (2023). The effectiveness of mindful hypnotherapy on psychological inflexibility, pain acceptance, headache disability and intensity in females with chronic migraine headache: A randomized clinical trial. *Life*, *13*(1), 131. https://doi.org/10.3390/life13010131

Olendzki, N., Elkins, G. (2017). Mindfulness and hypnosis. In G. R. Elkins (Ed.), *Handbook of medical and psychological hypnosis: Foundations, applications, and professional issues* (pp. 579-588). Springer Publishing Company.

Olendzki, N., Elkins, G. R., Slonena, E., Hung, J., & Rhodes, J. R. (2020). Mindful hypnotherapy to reduce stress and increase mindfulness: A randomized controlled pilot study. *International Journal of Clinical and Experimental Hypnosis*, *68*(2), 151–166. https://doi.org/10.1080/00207144.2020.1722028

Slonena, E. E., & Elkins, G. R. (2021). Effects of a brief mindful hypnosis intervention on stress reactivity: A randomized active control study. *International Journal of Clinical and Experimental Hypnosis*, *69*(4), 453–467. https://doi.org/10.1080/00207144.2021.1952845

Tang, Y.-Y., Hölzel, B. K., & Posner, M. I. (2015). The neuroscience of mindfulness meditation. *Nature Reviews Neuroscience*, *16*(4), 213–225. https://doi.org/10.1038/nrn3916

Chapter 18
Weight Management

MEREDITH VAGNER
CAMERON ALLDREDGE

Obesity is a multifaceted and growing public health concern across the globe, affecting a substantial portion of not only the adult population but the child and adolescent population as well. Just in the United States more than 2 in 5 adults can be considered obese, along with nearly 1 in 5 children and adolescents. This issue is not specific to the U.S. as global obesity rates have more than doubled for adults and quadrupled for children and adolescents in the last 35 years. Obesity is defined by a body mass index (BMI) of 30 or greater, and while it is not a perfect health measurement, BMI is a number derived from a calculation of height and weight that can help estimate your body fat composition. Online BMI calculators exist to help you determine whether obesity may be a concern for you.

One of the many reasons that obesity has garnered concern from physicians, health experts, and the public is its unequivocal ability to increase the risk for serious and sometimes life-threatening health issues. Conditions such as type 2 diabetes, high blood pressure, heart disease, stroke, metabolic syndrome, cancer, osteoarthritis, psychological disorders, and others can arise and become exacerbated by obesity. Obesity is the result of not only poor eating and drinking habits, a sedentary lifestyle (e.g., prolonged periods spent sitting in front of the TV or on personal electronic devices, working long hours without movement, less overall physical activity), or limited access to healthy foods, but from poor psychological health such as sustained stress over long stretches of time and unhelpful patterns of thinking. If the key to weight management was a simple "calories in, calories out" equation, then why has the problem worsened over time? What is at the heart of our global obesity struggle? The answer may lie in the lesser-known psychological elements contributing to obesity. In an effort to heal the body, the mind and the mind-body connection have often been neglected. Effective weight management strategies should help individuals to heal both the biological and psychological components influencing obesity and daily habits. First, let's take a look at healthy habits that can be integrated into a weight management treatment plan.

Lifestyle Changes for Weight Management

Many lifestyle changes are based on scientific research and can be used to aid weight loss, aside from more severe and invasive interventions like medication or bariatric surgery. Some of these changes include:

- Consume nutrient-dense whole foods and prioritize protein regularly.
- Limit processed foods, sugar, refined carbohydrates, and alcohol.
- Increase daily physical activity (e.g., walking, climbing stairs, lifting heavy objects around the house, general movement).
- Participate in strenuous exercise occasionally (e.g., lifting weights, sprints, push-ups).
- Establish a consistent sleep schedule.
- Avoid long, sedentary hours spent in front of screens.
- Break up extended periods of sitting with intermittent movement.

While these changes can be integral to one's weight management and leading a healthy life, they do not fully address the mental component of gaining weight that is typically ignored. Until the question of *why* you have difficulty maintaining healthy habits is explored, it may be difficult to stick to your health goals. Even if a person loses weight and picks up healthy habits, weight relapse can be common if the underlying psychology and emotions behind weight gain are not addressed. It's for this reason that lifestyle changes should be used in tandem with psychological interventions to both accelerate and maintain healing long-term. Hypnotherapy is one approach that has been researched and found to use the mind-body connection to effectively address psychological factors and help form healthy habits that can lead to better weight management.

What Does the Science Say About Hypnotherapy for Weight Management?

A recent meta-analysis synthesized the findings from several studies examining the effectiveness of hypnosis for weight loss when combined with cognitive-behavioral therapy (CBT). The analysis discovered that people who received CBT alone only lost 6 lbs. on average during treatment, while those who received both CBT and hypnosis lost nearly 12 lbs. on average by the end of treatment. Even more interesting, the individuals who received hypnosis and CBT continued to lose a considerable amount of weight over time while individuals who only received CBT plateaued. These findings suggest that hypnosis can help individuals not only lose weight in the short term but maintain their weight reduction long-term.

In two other meta-analyses, the effectiveness of hypnosis in the treatment of obesity and the impact of adding hypnosis to CBT were examined. In the first analysis, participants receiving hypnosis lost more weight than 94% of the participants not receiving hypnosis and about 81% more weight than other participants at their follow-up visits. In the second analysis, participants who received CBT alone were compared to participants who received CBT and hypnosis. Those treated with the combined CBT and hypnosis treatment lost more weight than 60% of the participants receiving only CBT and more than 79% of participants receiving only CBT at their follow-up visits.

A randomized controlled trial conducted in 2023 found that hypnosis, in combination with nutrition education, can help patients deal with obesity by improving their maladaptive coping strategies. After eight months of hypnotherapy, participants in the hypnosis group coped in less emotional and more task-oriented ways, decreased their distractibility, and had much more energy and less fatigue than participants who did not receive any hypnotherapy. This suggests that hypnosis, integrated with nutritional education and healthy habits, is a promising weight loss intervention that helps change the underlying coping behaviors contributing to overeating and weight gain.

Recent research has also investigated what happens when self-hypnosis is integrated into a person's lifestyle for weight management and overall health. Specifically, one study found that while clinician-directed hypnosis demonstrates measurable weight reduction, individuals who were taught self-hypnosis showed a greater reduction in caloric intake and weight loss. The same study found that self-hypnosis can promote satiety, increased quality of life, and decreased inflammation. In fact, the more frequently a person used self-hypnosis led to longer lasting weight loss and other positive benefits. So, if consistent hypnotherapy facilitated by a provider seems too daunting, self-hypnosis is a practical tool to utilize.

How Does Hypnotherapy Help with Weight Management?

Hypnosis is a helpful tool in treating obesity and managing weight due to its ability to bring about behavioral changes in addition to addressing emotional and psychological issues. Hypnosis for weight management usually includes hypnotic suggestions for relaxation, self-control, improved self-esteem, motivation, and stress relief. It can be used to help start or stop certain habits that are related to health and weight management. For example, hypnosis can help with the establishment and execution of regular physical exercise. Interestingly, it can also help to alter food cravings and general eating habits. When hypnosis is used in combination with healthy lifestyle practices and other psychotherapy approaches such as CBT, it is a powerful and effective method to manage weight and overall physical health.

Case Example – Lionel

Lionel was a 44-year-old male who worked a stressful job as a real estate broker. In an effort to cope with his stress, he often found himself eating sweets and junk food throughout the day and late into the night. His regular habit of exercising eventually fell apart, and he started to put on excessive weight. His poor physical health started to impact his functioning both at home and at work. Socializing became increasingly difficult and he felt depressive symptoms increasing as his anxiety continued to soar.

During one of Lionel's checkups, his physician informed him that making lifestyle changes to lose weight would be necessary if he wanted to improve his physical health. Lionel came and saw me (CA) to address his psychological and physical issues. We did regular psychotherapy and eventually introduced hypnosis in our sessions to help him with the needed changes. Hypnosis was used to help Lionel work through his anxiety symptoms and cultivate more relaxation and fulfillment in his day-to-day life. As his psychological symptoms became more manageable, we turned our attention to his eating and exercising habits.

With the use of hypnosis, we helped Lionel overcome initial mental blocks with his exercise and helped him to feel more satisfaction when he did exercise. Physical exercise was set up to feel as necessary as other daily habits like brushing his teething and reading the news. Simultaneously, we worked to alter his food cravings which involved hypnotic suggestions for healthier foods to seem more appealing and unhealthy food to taste bland and seem uninviting.

As Lionel was able to successfully implement the necessary lifestyle changes, he was able to lose the amount of weight suggested by his doctor. We continued our sessions for a while to help maintain his positive changes. There were occasions where excess stress at work led him to relapse into old habits, but these episodes were usually brief and minor. With practice and persistence, Lionel was able to adequately manage his anxious symptoms and established strong habits of exercise and healthy eating.

Summary

Obesity and weight concerns are an increasingly common and complex health issue affecting individuals across the world. Physicians often suggest weight loss to patients in an effort to prevent more serious health concerns. To maintain weight reduction over time, is it important to have an integrated approach, and we believe hypnosis can play an effective and key role in treatment. Hypnosis has been shown to be effective in the treatment of obesity, especially when it is used in combination with regular psychotherapy. Hypnosis helps with weight management by addressing underlying psychological issues and setting up habits consistent with healthy living.

REFERENCES

Bo, S., Rahimi, F., Goitre, I., Properzi, B., Ponzo, V., Regaldo, G., Boschetti, S., Fadda, M., Ciccone, G., Abbate Daga, G., Mengozzi, G., Evangelista, A., De Francesco, A., Belcastro, S., & Broglio, F. (2018). Effects of self-conditioning techniques (self-hypnosis) in promoting weight loss in patients with severe obesity: A randomized controlled trial. *Obesity*, *26*(9), 1422–1429. https://doi.org/10.1002/oby.2226.

Dulloo, A., & Montani, J. (2015). Pathways from dieting to weight regain, to obesity and to the metabolic syndrome: an overview. *Obesity Reviews*, 16. https://doi.org/10.1111/obr.12250

Elkins, G. (2022). Introduction to clinical hypnosis: The basics and beyond. Mountain Pine Publishing.

Kirsch I. (1996). Hypnotic enhancement of cognitive-behavioral weight loss treatments—another meta-reanalysis. *Journal of Consulting and Clinical Psychology*, *64*(3), 517–519. https://doi.org/10.1037//0022-006x.64.3.517

Milling, L. S., Gover, M. C., & Moriarty, C. L. (2018). The effectiveness of hypnosis as an intervention for obesity: A meta-analytic review. *Psychology of Consciousness: Theory, Research, and Practice, 5*(1), 29–45. https://doi.org/10.1037/cns0000139

Ramondo, N., Gignac, G. E., Pestell, C. F., & Byrne, S. M. (2021). Clinical hypnosis as an adjunct to cognitive behavior therapy: An updated meta-analysis. *The International Journal of Clinical and Experimental Hypnosis*, *69*(2), 169–202. https://doi.org/10.1080/00207144.2021.1877549

Sapp, M. (2017). Obesity and weight loss. In G. R. Elkins (Ed.), *Handbook of medical and psychological hypnosis: Foundations, applications, and professional issues* (pp. 589-597). Springer Publishing Company.

Untas, A., Lamore, K., Delestre, F., Lehéricey, G., Giral, P., & Cappe, E. (2023). Psychosocial effects of hypnosis in patients with obesity: A pilot randomized controlled trial. *American Journal of Clinical Hypnosis*, *65*(4), 281–298. https://doi.org/10.1080/00029157.2022.2152308

World Health Organization. (2024, March 1). *Obesity and overweight*. World Health Organization. https://www.who.int/news-room/fact-sheets/detail/obesity-and-overweight

Chapter 19
Coping with Cancer

VANESSA MUÑIZ

GARY ELKINS

Cancer affects over 19 million people per year, and there are over 32 million cancer survivors worldwide. It is estimated that over 40% of people will be diagnosed with cancer sometime during their lifetime. Breast cancer is the most common type of cancer among women, and men are more likely to have prostate cancers. Other types of cancer include lung cancer, colorectal, and liver cancer. However, cancer can occur anywhere in the human body. Treatments for cancer can result in side effects and add to the challenges in coping with cancer. In this chapter you will learn about the role of hypnotherapy in helping people to cope with cancer and to cope with the side effects that arise from cancer treatments.

Treatments for Cancer

A list of the most frequented treatments of cancer is provided below.

- Chemotherapy
- Hormone Suppressing Therapy
- Hyperthermia
- Immunotherapy
- Radiation Therapy

- Stem Cell Transplant
- Surgery

Symptoms Associated with Cancer Treatments

Cancer may go undetected, or it may cause considerable pain (especially if bone or nerve tissue is involved). Therefore, cancer screenings are very important. Research has shown that many cancer treatments, such as hormone suppression therapy, chemotherapy, and radiation can cause side effects and symptoms such as hot flashes, fatigue, and nausea, as well as pain and stress.

The diagnosis of cancer can be very stressful and lead to anxiety, sleep disturbances, and worry. One of the primary uses of hypnotherapy is in facilitating the relaxation response, reducing stress, and helping individuals cope with the uncertainty that is associated with cancer treatment prognoses. In addition, cancer related fatigue is also one of the most prevalent side effects of cancer care and treatment. In fact, more than 80% of cancer patients undergoing chemotherapy or radiation therapy experience fatigue before, during, or after their treatment. Fatigue can also be experienced because of stress after diagnosis. Although fatigue, tends to decrease as cancer treatment ends, it can persist months and even years post treatment. According to the National Institute of Health, symptoms that best characterize fatigue include:

- having difficulty moving, and/or thinking
- feelings of no energy due to physical, emotional, and mental exhaustion
- feeling extremely tired or lethargic.

Individuals experiencing stress and fatigue might also experience restlessness even after sleep.

Hot flashes are among the most distressing symptoms experienced by breast cancer survivors. Treatments for breast cancer (i.e., surgeries such as lumpectomies and mastectomies, hormone suppression therapy, aromatase inhibitors, tamoxifen and raloxifene), have been reported to cause significant, often overwhelming, amounts of hot flashes. Hot flashes are sudden and spontaneous sensations of intense heat, flushing, and sweating that tend to be accompanied by heart palpitations, fatigue, and anxiety. Hot flashes can cause a major decline in quality of life. Hypnotherapy has been shown to be an effective option for reducing hot flashes among breast cancer survivors (see Chapter 9 for more information).

Also, cancer-related pain is reported to occur in 50% or more of cancer patients across all cancer types. Cancer-related pain may be a symptom of the cancer itself or a side effect of treatments (e.g., chemotherapy, hyperthermia, surgery) or tests (e.g., biopsies or bone marrow aspirations). Pain can be a debilitating, disruptive symptom to patients in everyday life. Further, recent studies have found that about 31% of cancer patients are inadequately undertreated for cancer pain. Later in this chapter we will address how hypnotherapy can help with pain management.

Additionally, chemotherapy, hormone therapy, hyperthermia, immunotherapy, and radiation therapy all have been reported to cause nausea and vomiting. In addition to nausea and vomiting happening following treatment, cancer patients can experience *anticipatory nausea and vomiting,* which is defined by the National Cancer Institute as nausea and vomiting that occurs before a cancer treatment session begins. This occurs when a patient, having previously experienced nausea and vomiting after treatment, becomes triggered to feel these symptoms before the next session starts. Anticipatory nausea and vomiting occur in 70 to 80% of individuals treated for cancer and is characterized by having a significant impact on a patient's quality of life. Hypnotherapy can be an important consideration for anticipatory nausea and vomiting. Reports have shown that some patients may delay or discontinue future cancer treatments, primarily chemotherapy, due to the fear of further nausea and vomiting.

Hypnotherapy and Coping with Cancer

The American and Canadian Cancer Societies have endorsed hypnotherapy in the management of symptoms associated with cancer and side effects of cancer treatments. In a recent systematic review with over a dozen randomized clinical, controlled, trials with over 1,357 patients' results, found that hypnotherapy significantly reduced pain, distress, fatigue, and hot flashes (in breast cancer survivors). Hypnotherapy can help reduce symptoms and improve patients' quality of life and increase tolerance of treatments like chemotherapy and radiation. Thus, hypnotherapy is an important option for coping with the symptoms associated with treatment for cancer. These include the following:

- **Stress and Anxiety:** Undoubtedly, cancer is a stressful, and emotionally challenging time for the patient and loved ones. Almost all—if not all—hypnotherapy scripts include suggestions to foster a more positive outlook and reduce levels of stress and anxiety. For example, suggestions for strengthening of mental resilience empower patients through their cancer care journey. More specifically, mindfulness-based hypnotherapy can help patients cope with the emotional challenges of cancer, such as fear, depression, and feelings of helplessness. In a recent meta-analysis synthesizing the current literature available on stress management for cancer patients, studies found that patients' anxiety levels were significantly increased in control groups, remained the same in groups with empathic attention, and significantly decreased in the hypnosis intervention group. If you are interested in trying it out, Chapter 17 of this book offers a mindful hypnosis exercise you can practice as needed.

- **Hot Flashes in Breast Cancer Survivors:** Numerous treatments for breast cancer can cause hot flashes as a side effect. Hormone therapy (HT; estrogen alone or estrogen +

progesterone) is the most conventional treatment plan for the reduction of hot flashes and other vasomotor symptoms; however, breast cancer survivors might not qualify for HT due to estrogen sensitivity and higher risk of cancer recurrence (See Chapter 9 for more on hot flashes). This is why alternate treatment, preferably non-pharmacological, options are of high interest.

Hypnosis for hot flashes is highly effective. In a systematic review I (VM) have been working in preparation for my dissertation project (also focusing on hypnosis for hot flashes), hypnotherapy was found to be more effective in the reduction of hot flashes than comparator treatment groups such as structured attention controls, CBT, usual care, gabapentin, and venlafaxine. Not only that, but evidence also strongly and consistently showed that hypnosis achieved reductions greater than 50% across all studies. The figure below illustrates the findings of one of the randomized controlled trails with breast cancer survivors. In the study, hypnotherapy reduced hot flashes' frequency by 70% on average.

Hypnotherapy Reduces Hot Flashes

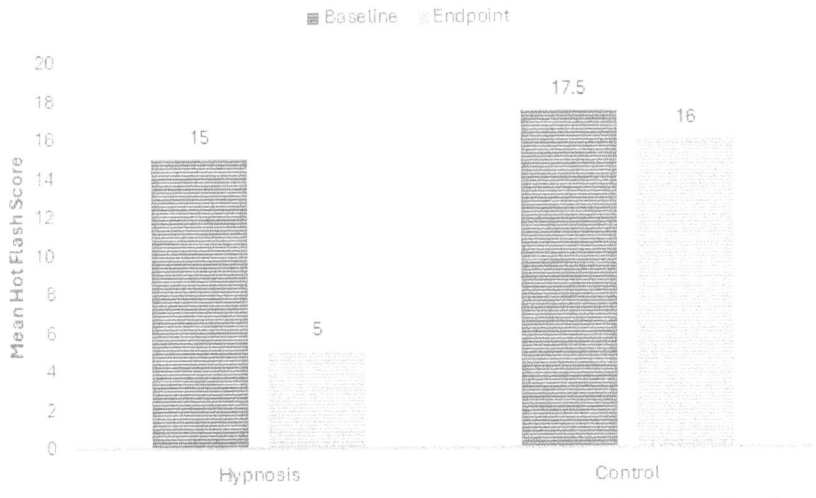

- **Cancer-Related Fatigue:** Numerous randomized clinical trials have strongly supported the evidence that hypnotherapy significantly reduces cancer-related fatigue. Given that fatigue is multi-dimensional, and presents itself differently at the individual level, it is usually measured using five dimensions of fatigue. These include general, physical, and mental fatigue (characterized by a lack of concentration), as well as reduced motivation and reduced activity. Reductions of fatigue are significantly lower across all dimensions with p-values ranging from $p = 0.002$ to $p < 0.001$, and effect sizes from 0.54 to 0.67. These findings are generally consistent across studies of diverse types of fatigue seen throughout different cancer types and treatments.

- **Pain Management in Cancer Patients:** Given its effectiveness and lack of side effects, hypnotherapy is one of the most recognized non-pharmacological treatments used for pain management across the general population. More recently, numerous studies have also found hypnotherapy to be an effective, and safe, non-pharmacological treatment for cancer-related pain. Systematic reviews report that in almost all randomized clinical trials, hypnosis interventions have had significant reductions in the intensity of the pain, regardless of the type of pain that is observed (i.e., acute or procedural pain from biopsies and related surgeries, or chronic pain). For example, in a randomized controlled trial on the effectiveness of hypnotherapy for chronic cancer pain, participants in the hypnotherapy group saw a reduction of over 50% in pain ratings at the 2-year follow-up. Moreover, in another study focusing on hypnotherapy for procedural pain from surgeries in breast cancer patients, participants assigned to the hypnosis treatment group reported less pain intensity on average (a score of 22.43 on a visual analog scale) compared to the control group (a score of 47.83).

- **Chemotherapy Related Nausea and Vomiting:** Based on our current understanding of hypnosis, we know that hypnotherapy improves anticipatory nausea and vomiting (ANV) by reducing treatment-related emotional distress and any response expectancy effects caused during previous chemotherapy sessions. Hypnotherapy has been recommended by the NIH's National Cancer Institute as an intervention for the prevention and treatment of ANV in chemotherapy. Published systematic reviews, meta-analyses, and clinical trials have consistently shown that hypnotherapy reduces ANV in children, adolescents, and adults, with a stronger recommendation for pediatric oncology.

How does Hypnotherapy Work to Help Cope with Cancer?

Hypnotherapy sessions typically span over several weeks and require daily hypnotic inductions geared towards offering suggestions that can mitigate the targeted symptoms (e.g., hypnotherapy for hot flashes is composed of daily interventions listened for five weeks in length). On the other hand, hypnotherapy for procedural, or acute, symptoms (i.e., surgical pain/ anesthesia) will require briefer and smaller quantities of hypnotic induction before, during, and after the procedure.

Suggestions might begin by anchoring the patient to a place where they feel the safest and most peaceful. This allows the patient to return to that safe space as needed. Hypnotic inductions typically conclude by suggesting continued comfort, strengthening mental resilience, or encouraging a speedy recovery: "Anything that is said to, or overheard by you that is less than helpful will be as if it is spoken in a foreign language. You are unable to understand it, and this will make it easier and more comfortable for you to succeed" (*Handbook of Medical and Psychological Hypnosis,* page 330).

Hypnotherapy also involves the practice of self-hypnosis. This is because self-hypnosis allows the patient to use hypnosis whenever they need to—whether they're anxious, in pain, and/or need to manage anticipatory nausea and vomiting. The self-hypnosis script below is an example on how it can be used for the management of anticipatory (adapted from the chapter by Alexander A. Levitan, *Nausea Associated with Chemotherapy* in the Handbook of Medical and Psychological Hypnosis).

> *"In a similar way, should you ever have any hint of queasiness, allow your finger and thumb to touch. This will instantly transport you to your favorite place of peace and comfort. Notice the tranquility, and beauty of that place. Any negative feelings will disappear, and any lingering feelings will be replaced by a special, pleasant taste in your mouth, whether that is mint, your favorite fruit, or any other flavor of your preference..."*
> (*Handbook of Medical and Psychological Hypnosis*, page 330).

Summary

Cancer treatments vary based on cancer type and stage. Strong evidence, primarily based on extensive research, has shown that hypnotherapy can be very helpful in coping with cancer related symptoms and improving the quality of life for cancer patients. Evidence is especially persuasive in regard to managing stress, reducing the number of hot flashes in breast cancer survivors, dealing with pain and fatigue, and coping with anticipatory nausea associated with chemotherapy. Hypnotherapy can be delivered by a trained professional (i.e., hypnotherapist) or it can be accessed using hypnotherapy apps (e.g., Evia app for hypnotherapy for hot flashes or the Finito app for smoking cessation). In self-hypnosis, the patient is empowered to manage cancer-related symptoms and stress.

REFERENCES

Brugnoli, M. P., Pesce, G., Pasin, E., Basile, M. F., Tamburin, S., & Polati, E. (2018). The role of clinical hypnosis and self-hypnosis to relief pain and anxiety in severe chronic diseases in palliative care: A 2-year long-term follow-up of treatment in a nonrandomized clinical trial. *Annals of Palliative Medicine*, *7*(1), 171-131. https://doi.org/10.21037/apm.2017.10.03

Elkins, G. R. (2016). *Handbook of medical and psychological hypnosis: Foundations, applications, and professional issues*. Springer Publishing Company.

Elkins, G., Marcus, J., Stearns, V., Perfect, M., Rajab, M. H., Ruud, C., ... & Keith, T. (2008). Randomized trial of a hypnosis intervention for treatment of hot flashes among breast cancer survivors. *Journal of Clinical Oncology*, *26*(31), 5022-5026. https://doi.org/10.1200/JCO.2008.16.6389

Greco, M. T., Roberto, A., Corli, O., Deandrea, S., Bandieri, E., Cavuto, S., & Apolone, G. (2014). Quality of cancer pain management: An update of a systematic review of undertreatment of patients with cancer. *Journal of Clinical Oncology*, *32*(36), 4149-4154. https://doi.org/10.1200/JCO.2014.56.0383

Lang, E. V., Berbaum, K. S., Faintuch, S., Hatsiopoulou, O., Halsey, N., Li, X., Berbaum, M. L., Laser, E., & Baum, J. (2006). Adjunctive self-hypnotic relaxation for outpatient medical procedures: A prospective randomized trial with women undergoing large core breast biopsy. *Pain*, *126*(1-3), 155-164. https://doi.org/10.1016/j.pain.2006.06.035

Montgomery, G. H., Bovbjerg, D. H., Schnur, J. B., David, D., Goldfarb, A., Weltz, C. R., Schechter, C., Graff-Zivin, J., Tatrow, K., Price, D. D., & Silverstein, J. H. (2007). A randomized clinical trial of a brief hypnosis intervention to control side effects in breast surgery patients. *Journal of the National Cancer Institute*, *99*(17), 1304-1312. https://doi.org/10.1093/jnci/djm106

Montgomery, G. H., Kangas, M., David, D., Hallquist, M. N., Green, S., Bovbjerg, D. H., & Schnur, J. B. (2009). Fatigue during breast cancer radiotherapy: An initial randomized study of cognitive–behavioral therapy plus hypnosis. *Health Psychology*, *28*(3), 317–322. https://doi.org/10.1037/a0013582

National Institute of Health (2024) *About Cancer*. National Cancer Institute. https://www.cancer.gov/about-cancer/

Sine, H., Achbani, A., & Filali, K. (2022). The effect of hypnosis on the intensity of pain and anxiety in cancer patients: A systematic review of controlled experimental trials. *Cancer Investigation*, *40*(3), 235-253. https://doi.org/10.1080/07357907.2021.1998520

van den Beuken-van Everdingen, M. H., van Kuijk, S. M., Janssen, D. J., & Joosten, E. A. (2018). Treatment of pain in cancer: Towards personalised medicine. *Cancers*, *10*(12), 502. https://doi.org/10.3390/cancers10120502

World Cancer Research Fund International (2024) *Worldwide Cancer Data.* https://www.wcrf.org/cancer-trends/worldwide-cancer-data/

Chapter 20
Coping with Medical Procedures

ALEX HOOD

CHRIS CORLETT

CAMERON ALLDREDGE

Approximately 64 million surgeries are performed in the United States each year. These can range in severity from pulling a tooth to an open-heart operation. Even though general anesthesia is common and relatively easy to access, surgical and other medical procedures can be experienced as disorienting, painful, confusing, and even frightening. Thus, there is a need for alternative methods of managing the distress and anxiety associated with these experiences, such as fear of pain, fear of not waking up after the procedure, or fear of waking up during the procedure. It is also well known that preoperative anxiety can lead to poorer recovery after the operation. Hypnosis has been shown to be especially effective at reducing patient pre- and post- medical procedure distress and anxiety. Additionally, in minimally invasive procedures, hypnosis can help reduce the amount of pain medication patients need to take afterward.

Coping with Medical Procedures – The Science

Medical professionals have studied how well hypnosis helps patients deal with a range of medical operations, surgeries, imaging procedures, biopsies (e.g., taking tissue for study), spinal taps (also called "lumbar punctures"), and more. Hypnosis has consistently been shown to reduce anxiety and distress that patients experience prior to and during medical procedures. For patients undergoing many minimally invasive procedures, hypnosis also reduces the amount of pain medication that patients need and may reduce the overall length of the procedure. Research has been conducted on hypnosis in the context of addressing things such as needle-related pain and discomfort, dental procedures, different types of surgeries, and the treatment of burn wounds.

Across a large number of studies, researchers have found that hypnosis can dramatically reduce children and adolescents' reported pain and distress for many of the most common reasons for needle sticks (e.g., inserting IVs, vaccine shots). Hypnosis is one of the most effective ways studied for reducing discomfort associated with needle-related procedures. Similarly, hypnosis has been shown to reduce pain in patients with severe burns and decrease their anxiety for painful burn-related medical operations. This is helpful when treating burns that require hospitalization because the intense pain can make regular cleaning and treatment of burn wounds difficult.

Dental procedures are often rated by patients as being highly distressing. However, there's strong evidence to show that hypnosis helps lessen peoples' distress during dental procedures better than any other non-drug treatment. In addition, studies show that pre-recorded audio hypnotic inductions work as well as inductions delivered in-person. This means that dental hypnosis can be very quick, easy, and convenient to induce.

Researchers have also investigated how well hypnosis helps patients deal with a variety of different serious medical procedures like heart surgery, eye surgery, plastic surgery, amputations, and more. Surgical procedures are very common, often cause patients severe distress, and are associated with several negative outcomes and side effects. Most studies look at hypnosis for operations where patients are awake but numbed (e.g., under *local anesthesia*), but many also look at procedures where patients are asleep (e.g., under *general anesthesia*). Across different types of surgery, the evidence shows that hypnosis helps lessen patients' distress and pain before *and* during procedures, lowers the amount of pain medicine patients need to take, shortens the duration of the operations, and speeds up patients' recovery. Looking in particular at patients undergoing minor breast cancer surgery, hypnosis also appears to reduce anxiety before the operation and lessen pain during recovery.

While most studies that investigate hypnosis for medical procedures examine its effects on adults, studies have shown that children and teens often experience even more benefit from hypnosis. It is hypothesized that this is because children and adolescents tend to have higher hypnotic ability, so they are able, on average, to see greater reductions in anxiety and pain during medical procedures. As mentioned previously, studies show that this is particularly true for children and teens undergoing needle-related medical procedures, with kids seeing dramatic reductions in pain and distress after hypnosis. Still, adults also experience significant benefit from hypnosis, with those who are more highly hypnotizable experiencing even stronger effects.

Case Example – Derek

Derek was an 11-year-old male with an intense fear of doctors and especially needles. This fear was severe enough to interfere with his ability to stay current on his routine vaccinations and prevented him from receiving important dental care. It became apparent that the distress he felt from the thought of getting a shot was much worse than the shot itself. Derek's parents tried a few different methods to help him, and ultimately found a clinician trained in hypnosis who agreed to see him.

Derek started to really enjoy his hypnotherapy visits. He went to a total of five sessions which were spent focused on reducing Derek's distress around needles and training him to reduce pain. With these sessions, he began feeling more empowered and confident in his ability to stay calm at the doctor's office. He was able to imagine that he was somewhere else entirely—a place that was comfortable and relaxing. He learned to alter sensations of pain to make them feel warm or cold, or numb them altogether. He liked the prospect of doing self-hypnosis whenever he needed to feel calmer.

By the end of treatment, Derek was able to close his eyes and repeat to himself some of the hypnotic suggestions given during their sessions such as:

- "My body is peacefully relaxing in my favorite place right now."

- "If I feel any discomfort on my body, I am able to send numbing cream to that spot which helps it feel numb and calm."

- "As I focus on my breathing, my body becomes more relaxed. My body will recover quickly which will let me focus on doing things I like to do."

When it came time to take Derek to his various appointments, his parents were shocked by how easily he engaged and how calm he was throughout the process. When it was time for the needle sticks, Derek closed his eyes, slowed down his breathing, and entered a state of peaceful relaxation like those experienced in his hypnotherapy sessions. At the dentist, he asked, "Has the shot happened yet?" (the part he was initially most worried about), to which the dentist chuckled and said, "That already happened about five minutes ago!"

Summary

Hypnotherapy is an effective treatment to help individuals prepare for and cope with medical procedures. Because medical procedures (especially those involving anesthesia) often lead people to experience high levels of distress and fear, a mind-body intervention is useful to manage those responses. Hypnosis has been shown to be effective in helping patients prepare for and cope with dental procedures, burn care, minor surgical procedures, fear of needles, and other pediatric care. While many adults have used hypnotherapy for these reasons, this use of hypnosis has been especially helpful for children.

REFERENCES

Birnie, K. A., Noel, M., Chambers, C. T., Uman, L. S., & Parker, J. A. (2018). Psychological interventions for needle-related procedural pain and distress in children and adolescents. *The Cochrane Database of Systematic Reviews, 10*(10), CD005179. https://doi.org/10.1002/14651858.CD005179.pub4

Burghardt, S., Koranyi, S., Magnucki, G., Strauss, B., & Rosendahl, J. (2018). Non-pharmacological interventions for reducing mental distress in patients undergoing dental procedures: Systematic review and meta-analysis. *Journal of Dentistry, 69,* 22–31. https://doi.org/10.1016/j.jdent.2017.11.005

Cheseaux, N., de Saint Lager, A. J., & Walder, B. (2014). Hypnosis before diagnostic or therapeutic medical procedures: A systematic review. *The International Journal of Clinical and Experimental hypnosis, 62*(4), 399–424. https://doi.org/10.1080/00207144.2014.931170

Darrow J.J. (2017). Explaining the absence of surgical procedure regulation. *Cornell Journal of Law and Public Policy. 27*(1), 189-206.

Fiddaman, J. (2016). Simple mastectomy under hypnosis: A case study approach. *Journal of Perioperative Practice, 26*(10), 217–220. https://doi.org/10.1177/175045891602601001

Flory, N., Salazar, G. M., & Lang, E. V. (2007). Hypnosis for acute distress management during medical procedures. *The International Journal of Clinical and Experimental Hypnosis, 55*(3), 303–317. https://doi.org/10.1080/00207140701338670

Holler, M., Koranyi, S., Strauss, B., & Rosendahl, J. (2021). Efficacy of hypnosis in adults undergoing surgical procedures: A meta-analytic update. *Clinical Psychology Review, 85.* https://doi.org/10.1016/j.cpr.2021.102001

Kekecs, Z., Nagy, T., & Varga, K. (2014). The effectiveness of suggestive techniques in reducing postoperative side effects: A meta-analysis of randomized controlled trials. *Anesthesia and Analgesia, 119*(6), 1407–1419. https://doi.org/10.1213/ANE.0000000000000466

Merz, A. E., Campus, G., Abrahamsen, R., & Wolf, T. G. (2022). Hypnosis on acute dental and maxillofacial pain relief: A systematic review and meta-analysis. *Journal of Dentistry, 123*, 104184. https://doi.org/10.1016/j.jdent.2022.104184

Noergaard, M. W., Håkonsen, S. J., Bjerrum, M., & Pedersen, P. U. (2019). The effectiveness of hypnotic analgesia in the management of procedural pain in minimally invasive procedures: A systematic review and meta-analysis. *Journal of Clinical Nursing, 28*(23-24), 4207–4224. https://doi.org/10.1111/jocn.15025

Provençal, S. C., Bond, S., Rizkallah, E., & El-Baalbaki, G. (2018). Hypnosis for burn wound care pain and anxiety: A systematic review and meta-analysis. *Burns: Journal of the International Society for Burn Injuries, 44*(8), 1870–1881. https://doi.org/10.1016/j.burns.2018.04.017

Rosendahl, J., Alldredge, C. T., & Haddenhorst, A. (2024). Meta-analytic evidence on the efficacy of hypnosis for mental and somatic health issues: A 20-year perspective. *Frontiers in Psychology, 14*, 1330238. https://doi.org/10.3389/fpsyg.2023.1330238

Schnur, J. B., Kafer, I., Marcus, C., & Montgomery, G. H. (2008). Hypnosis to manage distress related to medical procedures: A meta-analysis. *Contemporary Hypnosis, 25*(3-4), 114–128. https://doi.org/10.1002/ch.364

Tefikow, S., Barth, J., Maichrowitz, S., Beelmann, A., Strauss, B., & Rosendahl, J. (2013). Efficacy of hypnosis in adults undergoing surgery or medical procedures: A meta-analysis of randomized controlled trials. *Clinical Psychology Review, 33*(5), 623–636. https://doi.org/10.1016/j.cpr.2013.03.005

Zeng, J., Wang, L., Cai, Q., Wu, J., & Zhou, C. (2022). Effect of hypnosis before general anesthesia on postoperative outcomes in patients undergoing minor surgery for breast cancer: A systematic review and meta-analysis. *Gland Surgery, 11*(3), 588–598. https://doi.org/10.21037/gs-22-114

Chapter 21
Sports and Performance

ALEX HOOD

CAMERON ALLDREDGE

Sports are just as much mental contests as they are physical. While professional athletes spend countless hours training their bodies to reach peak performance, their mental preparation can often be the difference between winning and losing. Professional golfer Bobby Jones is quoted as saying, "Golf is a game that is played on a five-inch course—the distance between your ears." Mental training is essential for athletes in any sport to effectively translate their physical training into athletic performance. This is true especially at the upper echelons of competition, given the immense burden of performing in front of a crowd of spectators, the expectations placed upon athletes by themselves and others, and the small margin between victory and defeat.

Mental Training in Sports

Professional athletes at elite levels are at the pinnacle in terms of how well a person can do the action central to a given sport, such as shooting an arrow or throwing a ball into a net. Because of this, athletes at this level are, with few exceptions, nearly evenly matched. Across sports, winners and losers are often separated by thin margins. Even record-setting, standout athletes, like swimmer Michael Phelps, are not far ahead of their competition. When Phelps won the gold medal for the men's 100m butterfly in the 2008 Summer Olympics, his time was only half a second faster than the swimmer who finished in fourth place. This means that earning first place and failing to place were separated by half of a second. Given these incredibly close competitions, athletes do everything in their power to give themselves an "edge" over their opponents. Commonly, attempts to garner an advantage over fellow athletes may take the form of cheating or using performance-enhancing drugs. However, a strategy effectively employed by some athletes is the use of various techniques aimed at improving their mental performance—often referred to as *mental training*.

As a method of mental training, hypnosis has been used by famous athletes such as Tiger Woods, Nolan Ryan, and Michael Jordan. Woods famously uses self-hypnosis to achieve a state of relaxation during play, to minimize distractions, improve his concentration, and to visualize his swings before making contact with the ball. Nolan Ryan is said to have used hypnosis to achieve a "flow" state—a state where time seems to slow down, accompanied by a sensation that one's actions are occurring automatically—and to boost his confidence during games. Michael Jordan and many of his teammates on the Chicago Bulls used hypnosis before games to quell anxieties and to increase their focus during games. Across athletes who use hypnosis, many report it simultaneously enhances their ability to remain calm and improves their concentration.

How Hypnosis Helps and What the Science Says

Though highly effective in some domains, hypnosis is not a shortcut to superhuman athletic ability. There are nuances to understanding how hypnosis can help athletes' performance in different sports. In general, research on hypnosis for motivation, strength, and endurance has not found it to be more beneficial than suggestions or instructions delivered outside of hypnosis. Because sports are a diverse array of contests that draw on different skills, competencies, and physical abilities, hypnotic techniques are not equally useful for all athletes in all sports.

Intuitively, the physical training required for a high diver may bear no similarity to the training for a ski jumper. The same is true for the regimen of mental training best suited for each sport. Consequently, evidence suggests that hypnosis is most useful in improving performance for athletes in sports that require fine motor control and carefully coordinated movement—sports like golf, tennis, football, and soccer. Hypnosis appears to be less helpful for sports such as cycling, distance running, or cross-country skiing, which rely more on strength and physical endurance.

Moreover, within any given sport, different athletes face different challenges to optimum performance. An athlete's ability in a given sport (like basketball, for example) is made up of hundreds or thousands of smaller abilities (e.g., running, jumping, dribbling, shooting, passing, etc.). Each athlete will have a unique profile of relative strengths and weaknesses for the skills it takes to play their sport. A trainer hoping to improve an athlete's play will need to thoroughly understand their areas for improvement in order to help them.

In a similar way, athletes differ in the mental attributes that affect their performance. For example, some athletes may find that they perform best in low-pressure environments (e.g., during practice in a private area), while others notice their performance improves considerably in high-pressure environments (e.g., in front of a large crowd of spectators). Researchers refer to this idea as the *zone of optimal function*, which is different for each athlete. Before using hypnosis or any psychological intervention to improve performance for an athlete, it is important to understand where the athlete's "zone" is. Accordingly, for sport hypnosis to be effective, research suggests it must be individualized—this makes it challenging to study scientifically, because research trials typically rely on standardizing a single approach amongst a group of people to determine if it is effective.

Because clinical hypnosis is not a one-size-fits-all approach, it is helpful to consider the specific applications of hypnosis to improve sports performance that researchers have investigated. These include achieving a "flow state," improving concentration, increasing self-confidence, achieving relaxation, improving techniques, and maximizing the benefit of exercise. To begin, some researchers have identified "flow" as a hypnotic state achieved during the performance of a sport. Hypnosis interventions oriented toward helping athletes achieve a flow state have been found to be beneficial to performance among golfers and basketball players. Flow-specific interventions may also improve athletes' concentration. Studies support the helpfulness of specific post-hypnotic suggestions that reinforce focus and diminish the impact of distractions.

Enhanced self-confidence and relaxation are two other important applications of sport hypnosis. An athlete's beliefs about their own abilities, often referred to as *self-efficacy*, is one of the most important factors influencing their performance in a game. In general, those with higher self-efficacy perform better, work harder, and have more endurance than those who have low confidence in their abilities. In some studies, hypnotic techniques combined with reviewing videos of peak performance, feedback, imagery, and self-talk, have been shown to strengthen athletes' sense of self-efficacy and consequently improve performance. Improved self-efficacy has also been associated with decreased distraction for athletes who experience frequent negative thoughts during games. For athletes whose primary difficulty is obtaining enough rest between and before games, clinical hypnosis has been shown to considerably improve relaxation and lessen anxiety. Because elite athletes' schedules often leave little time for decompression between practices and performances, maximizing the benefit of downtime is critical. Hypnosis has been demonstrated as one of the most effective psychological relaxation techniques for athletes.

Hypnosis can also be used to help improve athletes' technique and aid in physical conditioning. Sports like golf, tennis, and baseball rely on athletes' ability to perform characteristic coordinated movements.

Properly swinging a club, a racquet, or a bat requires incredible precision, timing, detailed understanding of the ideal posture, and correct activation of the muscles involved in the movement. Often, problems occur somewhere in this complex sequence, resulting in an athlete's performance suffering from improper technique. Use of imagery, rehearsal in imagination, and other hypnotic tools have been shown to help athletes maintain proper technique across a variety of sports that rely on coordinated fine muscle movements. There is some evidence to suggest that hypnosis may also be beneficial in helping athletes detect subtle errors in complex movements, such as a golf swing, where identification of the problem can be a challenge. Studies also provide some evidence that hypnotic suggestions may be used to alter perceptions of exercise and physical conditioning. Suggestions that physical exertion will be perceived as pleasant, that muscle aches will be less noticeable, or that fatigue will be reduced, have been used to help improve the tolerability of intense exercise. Such methods are used with caution, however, since physical sensations of pain and exhaustion often bear important information about risk of injury.

Case Example – Marco

Marco was a highly accomplished golfer who competed at the collegiate level on one of the top golf teams in the country. Going into his junior year of college, he possessed all the skill and potential to be one of the best and strongest players on his team. However, his suboptimal performance in tournaments placed him in the bottom half amongst his teammates. His coach noticed that there was a big difference between how Marco played in practice and how he played during tournaments. His coach suggested that Marco meet with a psychologist to address any mental barriers that were preventing him from performing well at the times it was most important. Marco agreed and eventually found me (CA), and I suggested hypnotherapy as a potential avenue to improve his golf game.

In our first couple of sessions together, Marco and I identified that he plays very well in tournaments up until he makes a mistake. He indicated, "once I've made one mistake, I can't shake it off and I feel anxious about all of my future shots." This became a vicious cycle for Marco, because his anxious feelings usually interfered with his skill, which made him perform worse, which then led him to feel more anxious. Once we had identified this mental issue, we had to come up with an effective solution.

During one of our sessions together, Marco accidentally gave me an idea for something to try using hypnosis. Offhandedly, as he was talking about his mental block, he stated, "I just wish I could forget about any mistakes I make, and that my brain could move on as if it didn't even happen." I remember how perplexed he was when I responded with, "well, let's do that!"

Over the next few sessions, we used hypnosis to help Marco learn how to activate what we called a "mental reset." At the times he needed it, this allowed him to essentially erase (temporarily) the memory and experience of making a mistake, to reduce any unhelpful emotional and psychological reactions associated with the mistake. He was then able to tap into his well-established skills and technique to continue playing at his best, rather than being impeded by mental stress and worry. Of course, because it is helpful to learn from mistakes to know what to work on in practice, Marco was given the post-hypnotic suggestion that he could remember everything easily once the tournament was over.

This "mental reset" was incredibly helpful for Marco, as he used it any time he started to ruminate and worry about a previous mistake. He reported it gave him the mental clarity and confidence to rely more fully on the skills he had practiced so long and hard to establish. He even found that he could absorb and expand positive thoughts and feelings he experienced after making a great shot, which set him up with better energy for subsequent shots. He eventually finished the season with his best record and found himself leading the team by the end of their final tournament.

Summary

Clinical hypnosis to improve mental and physical performance in a given sport has been used by numerous professional athletes. Mental aspects of sports performance can be effectively addressed with clinical hypnosis. Specifically, hypnotherapy can be used to increase relaxation, facilitate a state of flow, improve coordination and technique, heighten focus, and alter perceptions of physical conditioning. While hypnosis won't give someone athletic skills they don't already possess, it is an effective tool for removing mental blocks that may be impeding access to practiced skills that have already been established.

REFERENCES

Barker, J. B., Jones, M. V., & Greenlees, I. (2013). Using hypnosis to enhance self-efficacy in sport performers. *Journal of Clinical Sport Psychology, 7*(3), 228–247. https://doi.org/10.1123/jcsp.7.3.228

Carlstedt, R. A. (2017). Sports Performance. In G. R. Elkins (Eds.), *Handbook of medical and psychological hypnosis.* (pp. 629-637). Springer Publishing Company.

Milling, L. S., & Randazzo, E. S. (2016). Enhancing sports performance with hypnosis: An ode for Tiger Woods. *Psychology of Consciousness: Theory, Research, and Practice, 3*(1), 45–60. https://doi.org/10.1037/cns0000055

Morgan, W. P. (2002). Hypnosis in sport and exercise psychology. In J. L. Van Raalte & B. W. Brewer (Eds.), *Exploring sport and exercise psychology* (2nd ed., pp. 151–181). American Psychological Association. https://doi.org/10.1037/10465-008

Onestak, D. M. (1991). The effects of progressive relaxation, mental practice, and hypnosis on athletic performance: A review. *Journal of Sport Behavior, 14*(4), 247–282.

Pelka, M., Heidari, J., Ferrauti, A., Meyer, T., Pfeiffer, M., Kellmann, M., (2016). Relaxation techniques in sports: A systematic review on acute effects on performance. *Performance Enhancement & Health.* 5(2), 47-59. http://dx.doi.org/10.1016/j.peh.2016.05.003

Taylor, J., Horevitz, R., & Balague, G. (1993). The use of hypnosis in applied sport psychology. *The Sport Psychologist*, *7*(1), 58-78. https://doi.org/10.1123/tsp.7.1.58

Unestahl, L. E. (2018). Alert, eyes-open sport hypnosis. *American Journal of Clinical Hypnosis*, *61*(2), 159-172. https://doi.org/10.1080/00029157.2018.1491387

Chapter 22
Flow State and Hypnosis

AARON FINLEY
CHRIS CORLETT
GARY ELKINS

Flow states are described by people from all walks of life. Everyone from athletes and artists to writers and video gamers have experienced and benefited from being in a psychological state called *flow*. As discussed in the previous chapter, an athlete may experience flow as effortlessly tuning in to the process of engaging with their mind and body for optimal athletic performance. For a ceramicist, the flow state may emerge when their hands and mind seem to be acting as one, without self-consciousness or indecision about what needs to happen to create the pot or sculpture they are working towards realizing. For a musician, the balance of their skills and the challenge of expressing themself may allow for flow states to infuse performances and improvisation with inspiration and soulfulness. For a writer, it may emerge in moments when writing becomes both a fluid process and a final product; when the writer can allow the words to appear on the page with great focus and purpose.

Hypnosis and Flow

Have you ever felt like you were "in the zone"? Maybe you've played tennis, been a dancer, or played an instrument for years, and then one day you notice yourself performing thoughtlessly, flawlessly without effort. Almost like the instrument was playing you. This is a state of intense absorption in which irrelevant things fade into the background of consciousness. This state of consciousness may be identified as a hypnotic state, as being in "a trance," or the flow state. There are many similarities between "flow" and the "hypnotic state" of consciousness.

Among the benefits of each may be a feeling of happiness and as a calm, focused state of awareness. A flow state experience may also include loss of self-consciousness, a sense of action and awareness merging, the transformation of time (i.e., time moving slowly or time flying due to focused engagement), an increased sense of control, extreme concentration on the task at hand, and autotelic experience (i.e., feeling of intrinsic joy and motivation to perform the activity).

Flow states offer many positive outcomes, one of which is reduction in anxiety. For musicians, this may show up as decreased music performance anxiety. Twin studies have shown that being prone to higher experiences of flow states has protective factors that decrease the likelihood of depression, anxiety, schizophrenia, bipolar disorder, and stress and cardiovascular diseases. Additionally, in his positive psychology research, Mihaly Csikszentmihalyi found that flow is sometimes connected to one's perceived quality of life. He theorized that challenge-skill balance, intrinsic motivation, and a loss of self-consciousness are all direct reflections of happiness. Therefore, flow state should result in happiness and continued engagement with the activity.

Achieving a "Flow State" with Hypnosis

As noted above, researchers have described some similarities between flow and the state of consciousness that occurs during self-hypnosis practice. In fact, as hypnosis is defined as "a state of consciousness involving focused attention and reduced peripheral awareness," the similarities are apparent as focused attention is a *primary* component of

Chapter 22: Flow State and Hypnosis

the flow state. Also, research has shown that there is a correlation between flow experience and how hypnotizable a person is.

A person who is high in hypnotizability is more likely to experience a flow state during hypnosis, and it is possible that hypnosis may be used to help people enter flow with higher frequency. People who are highly hypnotizable may experience greater losses of self-consciousness as well as higher levels of action-awareness merging and transformation of time. Hypnotic approaches to achieving a flow state may be especially useful for those who have difficulty accessing flow due to excessive negative self-talk.

One useful and interesting combination of hypnosis and flow is using hypnosis to induce people into a state of flow to improve athletic performance. Perhaps the best way to achieve enhanced athletic performance via flow state induced by hypnosis is through a three-state induction designed by Pates and his colleagues for a number of studies involving athletes in various sports, including golf performance. The example below illustrates this application.

Case Example – George

George was an elite-level European tennis player. He was young in his career and was looking for a way to improve his game. He was very strong technically but had trouble entering and maintaining the flow state, and he felt this was holding him back. He met some researchers who had been using hypnosis to see if they could help tennis players achieve a state of flow more easily, and George jumped at the chance.

The hypnosis intervention involved a number of stages. The first stage was progressive muscle relaxation. Second, once George was comfortable and relaxed, the hypnotherapist induced a hypnotic state. Third, George was asked to visualize previous flow experiences and his best competitive performances. The hypnotherapist asked George to recall as many sensory cues of those experiences as possible during this stage. Finally, the hypnotherapist introduced a natural trigger for re-experiencing these flow experiences and re-entering the flow state in the moment. In this case, the trigger was his tennis racket, and this association paired the activity with the flow state. Once George was re-alerted, the therapist assured that the trigger was well-paired. Following the in-person session, George was asked to listen to audio recordings at home to strengthen the association of the flow experience recall with the trigger object.

Aside from improving his standings in professional tournaments, George reported that he felt more relaxed on the tennis court and was having more fun playing the game. He also found that he had much greater control over his temper, an issue that had been plaguing him. All of this together made him feel more confident and capable of winning. Three weeks after the intervention, he had his first third-place finish.

Summary

The flow state is often the goal of any athletic or creative pursuit. It is the state one achieves when they combine a level of mastery of the skills required to perform the activity, heightened focus, and a lack of self-consciousness. When this occurs, an individual feels that they are at the "top of their game," that they are playing or performing as well as they ever have or could. It is when an individual does their best work. As both are considered states of focused attention and may involve reduced peripheral awareness, flow and hypnosis have a lot in common. There have been studies that show that hypnosis can be used to increase an individual's ability to enter the flow state. If you have trouble entering or maintaining the flow state but want to know what it feels like or want to take your craft to the next level, combining hypnosis and flow may help you achieve your goals.

REFERENCES

Bowers, J. (2017). Flow and peak experiences. In G. R. Elkins (Ed.), *Handbook of medical and psychological hypnosis: Foundations, applications, and professional issues* (pp. 559-563). Springer Publishing Company.

Carlstedt, R. A. (2004). *Critical moments during competition: A mind-body model of sport performance when it counts the most.* Psychology Press.

Cermakova, L., Moneta, G. B., & Spada, M. M. (2010). Dispositional flow as a mediator of the relationships between attentional control and approaches to studying during academic examination preparation. *Educational Psychology, 30*(5), 495–511. https://doi.org/10.1080/01443411003777697

Csikszentmihalyi, M. (1991). *Flow: The psychology of optimal experience.* HarperPerennial.

Csikszentmihalyi, M., & Csikszentmihalyi, I. S. (1992). *Optimal experience: Psychological studies of flow in consciousness.* Cambridge University Press.

de Manzano, Ö., Theorell, T., Harmat, L., & Ullén, F. (2010). The psychophysiology of flow during piano playing. *Emotion, 10*(3), 301–311. https://doi.org/10.1037/a0018432

Elkins, G. R., Barabasz, A. F., Council, J. R., & Spiegel, D. (2014). Advancing Research and Practice: The Revised APA Division 30 Definition of Hypnosis. *International Journal of Clinical and Experimental Hypnosis, 63*(1), 1–9. https://doi.org/10.1080/00207144.2014.961870

Gaston, E., Ullén, F., Wesseldijk, L. W., & Mosing, M. A. (2024). Can flow proneness be protective against mental and cardiovascular health problems? A genetically informed prospective cohort study. *Translational Psychiatry, 14*(1), 144.

Jackson, S. A., & Eklund, R. C. (2002). Assessing flow in physical activity: The flow state scale-2 and dispositional flow scale-2. *Journal of Sport and Exercise Psychology, 24*(2), 133–150. https://doi.org/10.1123/jsep.24.2.133

Lindsay, P., Maynard, I., & Thomas, O. (2005). Effects of hypnosis on flow states and cycling performance. *The Sport Psychologist, 19*(2), 164–177. https://doi.org/10.1123/tsp.19.2.164

Moral-Bofill, L., López de la Llave, A., Pérez-Llantada, M. C., & Holgado-Tello, F. P. (2022). Development of flow state self-regulation skills and coping with musical performance anxiety: Design and evaluation of an electronically implemented psychological program. *Frontiers in Psychology, 13*, 899621.

Nakamura, J., & Csikszentmihalyi, M. (2005). The concept of flow. In C. R. Snyder & S. J. Lopez (Eds.), *Oxford handbook of positive psychology* (pp. 89–105). Oxford: University Press.

Pates, J., Cummings, A., & Maynard, I. (2002). The effects of hypnosis on flow states and three-point shooting performance in Basketball players. *The Sport Psychologist, 16*(1), 34–47. https://doi.org/10.1123/tsp.16.1.34

Pates, J. (2013). The effects of hypnosis on an elite senior European tour golfer: A single-subject design. *International Journal of Clinical and Experimental Hypnosis, 61*(2), 193–204. https://doi.org/10.1080/00207144.2013.753831

Payne, B. R., Jackson, J. J., Noh, S. R., & Stine-Morrow, E. A. (2011). In the zone: Flow state and cognition in older adults. *Psychology and Aging, 26*(3), 738–743. https://doi.org/10.1037/a0022359

Seger, J., & Potts, R. (2012). Personality correlates of psychological flow states in videogame play. *Current Psychology, 31*(2), 103–121. https://doi.org/10.1007/s12144-012-9134-5

Chapter 23
What Is Stage Hypnosis And How Does It Work?

CAMERON ALLDREDGE

The term "stage hypnosis" refers to the use of hypnosis for entertainment. It is typically done by an individual who presents themselves as a *hypnotist* and calls volunteers from the audience to join them (usually on a stage) and provides entertainment. Most hypnosis shows follow a similar format where the hypnotist attempts to educate the audience on hypnosis and then fills empty seats lining the stage with willing subjects who undergo some type of hypnotic induction followed by a series of suggestions of silly, bizarre, and even embarrassing tasks ending only when the hypnotist decides to "wake them up" at the conclusion of the show. To many, it is thoroughly enjoyable to watch friends and strangers behaving as if under the influence of another person who can command them to do abnormal things.

Writing as someone who used to do this sort of thing, I would be happy to inform you about stage hypnosis and how it works. Let me start by saying that stage hypnosis is no hoax. It works through the same principles used for hypnotherapy but for purposes less noble. I can assure you that volunteers are not planted into the audience with orchestrated plans to trick the observers. Instead, the hypnotist and their subjects are usually strangers to each other. However, most stage hypnotists are careful to maximize their likelihood for success by selecting the best candidates (I'm not at all suggesting that there's a valid way to know that someone is highly hypnotizable just by observing them or talking to them—if there is something like that, we haven't found it yet). Getting good candidates is actually pretty simple because they are usually the ones who quickly volunteer to come up on stage. The act of going on stage is already an "unspoken agreement" between the hypnotist and volunteer because they are actively providing their consent for the hypnosis. In addition, going on stage creates a strong expectation that hypnosis will happen, and this interacts with a strong desire to appear as a good candidate to the audience.

So, stage hypnosis creates a perfect storm with high expectations, maximized willingness, and good probability that volunteers will have high hypnotizability. From there, the hypnotist provides a hypnotic induction and subsequent suggestions designed to produce entertaining responses. Many people (especially skeptics) like to assume that volunteers are just *acting*. I believe it is much more accurate to realize that they are simply *reacting*. In other words, they are genuinely reacting to the new circumstances suggested by the hypnotist. Because their rational and analytic thinking is reduced (see Chapter 2), volunteers have what feels to them to be a very real experience. As a result, the audience often finds the volunteers' reactions to the experience entertaining.

For example, if someone experiencing hypnosis is given the suggestion that their shoe has turned into a phone, that obviously doesn't happen in reality; but, it does seem completely real in *their* reality. All of the sudden, they begin to experience their shoe ringing with an incoming call because that seems real and valid to them, and their mind is able to produce that experience. The audience finds this amusing because they observe someone holding their shoe up to their face having a full conversation with it. Again, the best way to think about stage hypnosis is the volunteers are *reacting* to new circumstances that are, by nature, entertaining to observe.

Chapter 23: What Is Stage Hypnosis and How Does It Work?

Summary

Stage hypnosis is the use of hypnosis for the purpose of entertainment. With advantages such as expectancy, willingness, and high hypnotizability, stage hypnotists utilize similar techniques and principles as those found in hypnotherapy. What audience members witness is a group of volunteers reacting to strange, new circumstances suggested by the hypnotist. In essence, the hypnotic suggestions can become their new reality. Depending on the nature of the suggestions, the behavior of the volunteers can seem bizarre and uninhibited (which is exactly why stage hypnosis can be so entertaining).

Chapter 24
Beginning Hypnotherapy and Additional Resources

CAMERON ALLDREDGE
VICTOR JULIAN PADILLA

Once a person understands the many applications of hypnotherapy and has interest in using it for their own life, it's important to know how to best begin hypnotherapy. There are essentially three options: begin by using a hypnotherapy app, see a clinician who practices hypnotherapy, or a combination of the two. If you decide to seek a clinician who practices hypnotherapy, your search will likely depend on what issues you want treated. You may see a clinician in person or virtually (yes, hypnosis can work just as well over videoconferencing or phone calls as it does in face-to-face sessions). Your success with hypnosis will depend a lot on your own ability and practice with self-hypnosis audio recordings, rather than only depending on the skill of a hypnotherapist. With that said, here are three helpful things to keep in mind when selecting a professional to work with:

#1 Find someone you feel you can trust.

Trust between a hypnotherapist and patient is an essential ingredient for successful hypnotherapy. It's obviously going to be difficult to let go and have a full experience when you don't truly trust the other person in the room. Hypnosis can feel vulnerable with your eyes closed and in a reclined body position, so it is crucial that you have established a healthy bond beforehand. A good hypnotherapist will work to establish a trustworthy relationship with you from the start. Keep in mind that it's normal to need a few sessions with a therapist before you feel that you can fully trust them and be open.

#2 Find someone who is trained to treat your concern.

Similar to the broader field of mental health, different problems require different levels of care and different types of professionals. Life coaches may be well equipped to help with common challenges (such as mild to moderate stress or adjusting to new circumstances), while some issues may require treatment from a psychologist or licensed therapist with more specialized training. The same principle applies to hypnosis. So, your search for a hypnotherapist depends greatly on your goals for treatment. When trying to figure out where to look, a helpful question to ask yourself is, "If I were to get my issue treated by someone who does not use hypnosis, what type of professional would I seek out?" Based on how you answer that question, you can narrow your search to certain types of professionals who have hypnosis training.

*#3 Find someone who focuses on **positive** changes.*

A good hypnotherapist will use sessions to focus on what you want rather than what you don't want. The likelihood of success is lower if sessions focus on "getting rid of" a habit or symptom that is undesirable. The positive outcome and its associated effects should be the foundation of hypnosis sessions. You can expect to walk away from most hypnotherapy sessions feeling hopeful, determined, and empowered.

Finally, it is important to emphasize the practice of self-hypnosis. Even if someone is meeting with a therapist on a weekly basis, it is highly beneficial to implement regular and formal practice of self-hypnosis. This may include use of a hypnotherapy app, such as those from Mindset Health, listening to an audio track, or simply taking time to relax in a comfortable place and return to a similar state of consciousness with intent to re-experience the suggestions that were provided in sessions. Either way, the consistent and deliberate practice of self-hypnosis can be extremely helpful and an essential part of hypnotherapy.

Additional Resources

Digital Hypnotherapy and Hypnosis Apps

If you want to begin with using a hypnotherapy app, some evidence-based options are the digital hypnotherapy apps from Mindset Health. Mindset Health is a leader in hypnotherapy apps and works to develop science-based apps that deliver clinical hypnosis programs for consumers interested in hypnotherapy. Mindset Health has apps specifically designed to manage issues such as chronic back pain (Relio), smoking cessation (Finito), depression and anxiety (Claria), hot flashes (menopausal and for breast cancer survivors; Evia), and IBS (Nerva) with more apps planned for future release. Dr. Elkins has an interest in Mindset Health and serves on the scientific advisory board along with other well-known and respected experts in clinical hypnosis. More information on Mindset Health and their available hypnosis apps can be found at mindsethealth.com/hypnotherapy and the apps are available for download in the Apple App Store or the Google Play Store.

Another excellent app for digital hypnosis is *Mesmerize* developed by the team at Pzizz. Mesmerize features a vast library of hypnosis tracks and guided meditations with new content being added regularly. It contains hypnosis audio presets for goals like falling asleep, relaxation, lucid dreaming, improving focus, enhancing confidence, stress relief, and overcoming fears. It uniquely integrates captivating visuals that can be used to enhance focus and relaxation. One of the advantages of Mesmerize is the powerful customization options that gives users control over the length of sessions, background music, and timers. Dr. Alldredge has an interest in Mesmerize and serves as a creator for much of the hypnosis content. More information on Mesmerize can be found at mesmerizeapp.com and the app is available for download in the Apple App Store and the Google Play Store.

Podcast Episodes

"Dr. Gary Elkins—Recent Hypnosis Research" by *Center Point Radio*

"Clinical Hypnosis Research with Dr. Gary Elkins, PhD" by *Psychology Talk Podcast*

"Dr. David Spiegel: Using Hypnosis to Enhance Mental & Physical Health & Performance" by *Huberman Lab*

Articles

"How Hypnosis Works, According to Science" in *Time* https://time.com/6171844/how-hypnosis-works/

"Uncovering the New Science of Clinical Hypnosis" in APA's *Monitor on Psychology* https://www.apa.org/monitor/2024/04/science-of-hypnosis

"Hot Flash Help for Women Who Can't Do Hormone Therapy" in *Oprah Daily* https://www.oprahdaily.com/life/health/a60719562/hot-flash-help-for-menopausal-women/

Books for Clinicians

The following works cover perspectives on clinical hypnotherapy. Many of the books by Dr. Gary Elkins and Dr. Michael Yapko include session-by-session instructions, timelines, measures, and how clinicians can incorporate hypnotherapy into their clinical practices.

Elkins, G. R. (2017). *Handbook of medical and psychological hypnosis: Foundations, applications, and professional issues.* Springer Publishing.

Chapter 24: Beginning Hypnotherapy and Additional Resources

Elkins, G. R., & Olendzki, N. (2019). *Mindful hypnotherapy: The basics for clinical practice.* Springer Publishing.

Elkins, G. R. (2022). *Introduction to clinical hypnosis: The basics and beyond.* Mountain Pine Publishing.

Hammond, D. C. (1990). *Hypnotic suggestions and metaphors.* W.W. Norton & Company

Milling, L. S. (2023). *Evidence-based practice in clinical hypnosis.* American Psychological Association.

Raz, A., & Lifshitz, M. (2016). *Hypnosis and meditation: Towards an integrative science of conscious planes.* Oxford University Press.

Yapko, M. D. (2011). *Mindfulness and hypnosis: The power of suggestion to transform experience.* W. W. Norton.

Yapko, M. D. (2019). *Trancework: An introduction to the practice of clinical hypnosis* (5th ed.). Routledge.

Yapko, M. D. (2021). *Process-oriented hypnosis: Focusing on the forest, not the trees.* W. W. Norton & Company.

Academic Journals

If you are curious to learn more about the evidence behind hypnotherapy, the journals listed here are a great resource for getting regular updates on the latest hypnotherapy research across the globe. For most of these journals, collaborations with national and international clinical and experimental hypnosis associations are common, so interested readers are able to also get a glance at current publications, presentations, or special issues from conferences hosted by these organizations.

International Journal of Clinical and Experimental Hypnosis
https://www.tandfonline.com/toc/nhyp20/current

American Journal of Clinical Hypnosis
   https://www.tandfonline.com/journals/ujhy20

Psychology of Consciousness: Theories, Research, and Practice
   https://www.apa.org/pubs/journals/cns

Concluding Remarks

As stated in our introduction, our goal for this book was to write it based on the science but in a way that can be easily read by the general public—an academic resource written in a non-academic style. Our hope in doing this is to shed some light on the reality and benefit of a therapeutic tool that is so often clouded by mystery and misinformation. To accomplish this, we have covered what hypnosis is, how it works, the scientific evidence, and some of its diverse applications. We have also provided information regarding sessions of hypnotherapy, stage hypnosis, how to find a hypnotherapist, and additional resources for deeper exploration.

Some of the main takeaway points we hope readers glean from these pages include:

- Hypnosis is a state of consciousness involving three things: focused attention, reduced peripheral awareness, and an increased ability to respond to suggestions.

- Hypnosis is not something that is done to you, it is something you learn to do.

- Past scientific research has identified parts of the brain (the default mode network, the salience network, and the executive control network) that are involved in the experience of hypnosis.

- Hypnotherapy often helps by harnessing the relaxation response, influencing the mind-body connection, improving one's ability to respond to helpful ideas, facilitating insight, and communicating with the unconscious mind.

- Successful hypnotherapy relies heavily on specific, change-oriented goals.

- Hypnotherapy is safe and often reported to be a pleasant experience.

- Scientific research on hypnosis has been occurring for decades and at institutions like Stanford University and Baylor University.

- Hypnotizability can be viewed as a talent that everyone possesses to varying degrees. Things like intelligence, creativity, and ability for absorption are correlated with higher levels of hypnotizability.

- When searching for a hypnotherapist or clinician who uses hypnotherapy, consumers are encouraged to find someone they feel they can trust, find someone trained to treat their concern, and find someone who focuses on positive changes.

- Hypnotherapy is well researched and used for concerns that include (but are not limited to)
    » Insomnia
    » Phobias
    » PTSD
    » Hot flashes
    » Stress and anxiety
    » Depression
    » Irritable Bowel Syndrome
    » Chronic pain
    » Weight management

- » Smoking cessation
- » Coping with medical procedures

- Self-hypnosis is a powerful tool that anyone can learn to use. There are apps available (like the Mesmerize app and those from Mindset Health) that can help with self-hypnosis.

Ultimately, we are passionate about the scientific exploration and therapeutic use of hypnosis because we have seen it facilitate profound changes in people's lives countless times. As the title of this book suggests, it is our hope that you have a deeper understanding of hypnosis and hypnotherapy with enough access to "what you need to know" to begin using it in your personal life. We are excited for anyone who embarks on a journey to improve their life through this potent method of psychological and behavioral change.

About the Authors

Dr. Gary Elkins is a Professor of Psychology and Neuroscience at Baylor University and the Director of the Mind-Body Medicine Research Laboratory where he conducts research into hypnosis for stress, sleep, trauma, smoking cessation, and hot flashes. Dr. Elkins is the leading researcher and expert on hypnosis for hot flashes and sleep disturbances as well as other clinical applications. His research into hypnosis interventions has been funded by NIH grants for over 20 years. Dr. Elkins is the Editor-in-Chief of the *International Journal of Clinical and Experimental Hypnosis*. Dr. Elkins is Past-President of the Society for Clinical and Experimental Hypnosis, the American Society of Clinical Hypnosis, the Division of Psychological Hypnosis of the American Psychological Association, and Past-President of the American Board of Psychological Hypnosis. He has received the American Society of Clinical Hypnosis Wall Award for Excellence in Teaching Clinical Hypnosis. He is diplomate of the American Board of Clinical Health Psychology (ABPP) and the American Board of Psychological Hypnosis. Dr. Elkins has over 100 publications which include books: *Handbook of Medical and Psychological Hypnosis: Foundations, Applications, and Professional Issues*; *Mindful Hypnotherapy: The Basics for Clinical Practice; and Introduction to Clinical Hypnosis: The Basics and Beyond.* In association with Mindset Health, Dr. Elkins has assisted in the development of two hypnosis apps: the *Finito* app for smoking cessation and the *Evia* app for hot flashes/sleep. In recognition of his research, Dr. Elkins has received major awards: the Society of Behavioral Medicine's *Complementary and Integrative Medicine Investigator Research Award*, and the *Distinguished Contribution to Science Award* from Division 30 of the American Psychological Association. He is an Adjunct Professor at Texas A&M

University College of Medicine and a Medical Associate with Baylor Scott and White Hillcrest Medical Center.

Dr. Cameron Alldredge is a licensed psychologist and associate research scientist in the Mind-Body Medicine Research Laboratory at Baylor University. He teaches psychology classes on both an undergraduate- and graduate-level and runs a small private practice that focuses on hypnotherapy and non-ordinary states of consciousness. Dr. Alldredge has received multiple awards including APA Division 30's recognition for ground-breaking early career contributions to the advancement of scientific hypnosis and the *Stanley Krippner Award* from the Society for Clinical and Experimental Hypnosis. He has published dozens of scientific articles on clinical hypnosis and has led countless workshops and trainings for the Society for Clinical and Experimental Hypnosis and the American Society of Clinical Hypnosis.

www.ingramcontent.com/pod-product-compliance
Lightning Source LLC
Chambersburg PA
CBHW050109170426
43198CB00014B/2504